SURVIVAL QUEST

TRUE STORIES OF HOW THE
ORDINARY DO THE EXTRAORDINARY

SALLY DEMASI

Dr. Cottingham —
Thanks for our Journey —

Sally DeMasi
7.17.17

*This book is dedicated to the spirit of Michael,
one of my best friends and guides.*

∽

SURVIVAL

The result of conquering a difficult
physical or emotional situation with a
doubtful outcome. The act of challenging
and overcoming, leading to growth.

ADVENTURE

A trip to the unknown. An intimate
relationship with life that produces
passion, mystery, and magic.

∽

~

Our fate is determined by how far we are prepared to push
ourselves to stay alive—the decisions we make to survive. We
must do whatever it takes to endure and make it through alive.

Bear Grylls

Life is daring adventure, or nothing.

Helen Keller

What allows us, as human beings, to psychologically
survive life on earth, with all of its pain, drama, and
challenges, is a sense of purpose and meaning.

Barbara de Angelis

A man's pride can be his downfall, and he needs to learn
when to turn to others for support and guidance.

Bear Grylls

Until you dig a hole, you plant a tree, you water it and make
it survive, you haven't done a thing. You are just talking.

Wangari Maathai

Survival can be summed up in three words—never give up.

Bear Grylls

My mission in life is not merely to survive, but to thrive; and to do so
with some passion, some compassion, some humor, and some style.

Maya Angelou

The line between life or death is determined
by what we are willing to do.

Bear Grylls

~

Contents

Introduction

HAVE YOU EVER WONDERED HOW YOU would find your way if you were lost, whether you would have the emotional strength to resolve an emergency that could be your last on earth, or if you could endure situations you never expected? I have. I began writing this book with the hope of solving these puzzles by sharing the experiences of ordinary people who did the extraordinary.

I love taking risks. Life to me is one big adventure, which has certainly included some risky parts. Some were larger and more threatening than others, but I have a way of finding danger anywhere I go. It has been that way since I could walk; I strove for the unusual and explored as far from home as Mom would let me. When I was older, I had the aid of a car, a plane, a boat, and longer legs, so I could venture farther, eventually going to the ends of the world where I explored cultures, danger, and my mantra: risk.

In my early college years, I discovered art (and men) in Siena, Italy, which fed my desire for travel and creativity. The day after graduating, I packed my car and left for a paradise I was sure existed on the opposite side of the country: California.

It would be as amazing as all the movies and TV shows I watched.

It didn't disappoint.

But my introduction to paradise was a cockroach-filled room. After driving twenty-five thousand miles across the U.S. in my tiny VW to create a new me—the authentic me, with no boundaries—I dropped my bags full of hopes and childhood memories at a men's flophouse, the Wilshire Apartments, in Hollywood, California. With little money, I needed to start my life—pronto. I had a strong commitment to make this transformation a reality. Wasn't I all grown up, a woman of the world in this glittery state, free to do and become anything I wished? I could begin risking full bore.

Looking back on that scene, I recognize that I was about to enter the survival game.

I lived in a bad part of Hollywood, and streetwalkers crossed my path outside the cheap café where I ordered my daily meal of soup, with lots of crackers to fill me up. I survived by listening to my instincts. I learned when to leave in order to avoid a dangerous situation, and when to trust my new acquaintances to enrich my life.

I never gave survival a second thought; the young don't. On my first flight to Europe, our plane encountered some mechanical problems along with unusually strong turbulence. I looked at the other passengers, most holding the arms of loved ones. I was traveling alone—I *always* travel alone, mostly because I want to be in control of my own destiny. For a second on that flight I speculated on the chances that we'd crash. My young life would be over. Yet I never thought about survival. I felt protected, invincible; nothing could happen to me.

Wrong, I realized as I matured.

Decades later, in my fifties, I had a similar experience on a flight from Africa to Europe. My perspective had changed. I'd learned that I could be vulnerable in crisis situations, even die. I'd learned that it even happens to people who are not knowingly challenging life. Many on that plane were on holiday; I'd just completed part of my adventure in Africa, existing in another culture, alone, on the streets of Nairobi. It had been frightening, but also challenging. Locals stared, warned me to take a taxi, and told me about the thieves who cut off fingers for the rings. I wasn't wearing any.

I was old enough to be scared for my life, but at that time I was intentionally searching for courage to conquer my fears and grow. I needed to live in Nairobi on my own and prove it was within me.

I survived, and had made it to a safe place—an airplane bound for one of my favorite parts of the world, Italy, where I would take a well-earned rest from my risking.

As we flew over the ocean, something went wrong, resulting in a frightening plunge. The passengers were told an engine was "nonfunctional": we needed to land immediately. There was commotion and then an eerie silence, a resignation to whatever might happen. Surrender.

Not for me. I quickly processed what might happen next. I would be prepared.

I scanned and saw a few lights below in the blackness. As we continued our path almost straight down, the lights below rapidly multiplied—a city. I remember being thankful we would not land in the ocean somewhere between Nairobi and Rome.

Death was possible, but I would fight with whatever little control I had in my realm. I quickly removed medicine from my backpack, papers to prove my citizenship, and my comforting family pictures, and stuffed them into my safari vest. I did one, rather weird last thing, but felt compelled in that moment: I changed from my fashionable leather heels, which I'd put on for Italy, into my hiking boots. I would hit the ground running. I would survive.

Our plane landed that night in Cairo, where another adventure ensued, but that is described in my previous book, *Courage Quest.*

Only later did I realize how my perspective had changed about danger and survival from that previous flight in my younger years.

I've managed to have an amazing life full of trials, creative endeavors, and wanderings. I've taken the corporate world to developing nations, where technology clients just didn't want to follow my project management schedules. Each venture has been bold, often unusually risky, and full of undiscovered danger that I confronted face on.

For me, surviving means conquering a difficult physical or emotional situation while doubting the outcome. You challenge yourself, and through mental and emotional strength, you overcome. You realize, sometimes shocked, that your heart is still beating and you are still with the living. When the adrenaline is pumping, you feel larger than life and less afraid of anything, and that feeling amazingly carries forward to help you grow and actualize all you can be.

Survivors don't tiptoe through life; we live it with gusto.

My life is predicated on adventures, which has led me to this question about survival. I have moved into unknown territory, settled in new places, tackled jobs I had no background for, and strove to be the best performer.

An adventure is delighting in the unknown and tasting the total, unproven experience. That involves risking and learning. Anything can be an adventure if you have an open mind and the attitude of exploration. It produces passion, mystery, and magic. These were always components in my life, but later I ratcheted them up a notch and started what I call *extreme adventures*. These were not ordinary "vacations." I set out on these solo trips to little-known places on our globe to see if I could make it on my own, and to test my courage.

I explored the outdoors through rafting, kayaking, and camping in bear-infested lands, often alone. I traveled all over the world by myself to feel the cultural diversity and experience how others live with little money or government support.

Frequently, I encountered threats and had to overcome. I was challenged by walking the streets of Nairobi and drug-infested areas of Athens. I discovered camping in the desert of Kenya, surrounded by wildlife, and slept in a tree house in a hippie-filled area of Turkey. I psychologically confronted who I was and how I could interact with fear and move on.

As I started searching for answers, I saw that fear, and the way we handle it, is a large component in surviving. After fifteen years, I have found my peace. I uncovered, at least for me, the basis of survival: confronting crises with courage and using the resources I've accumulated during my life to survive and flourish.

Adventuring alone and then writing about the challenges in my first book were no longer enough. I wanted to examine what it would take to move forward in life, and to experience what might be called "my last adventures." This would be different than in the past.

I played with this concept for years in my mind, and then I started reading stories and talking to people about their unique experiences. I eventually began to question strangers as I tried to uncover why some people live and others don't in a crisis situation. I became brazen in my quest for answers. It became an obsession to find a survival road map for the future.

What I discovered was that most books about outdoor adventure, risk, and survival were almost exclusively written by men, about men, and targeted to men, while the books on emotional survival were for and about women. I want to change that.

In my writings I discuss events of ordinary people like you and me. I've found both male and female examples of those who have faced fear and physical risk. They were kayaking in an extreme location, exploring backcountry, paragliding, discovering, and *surviving*. I explored emotional upheaval and medical experiences you just shouldn't live through. Those human stories are now my heroic guides toward the future.

How do people navigate the tough stuff life throws at us? Some people confront their situations with passion, making their best effort to succeed—and some do not. Why?

I found answers.

The more I searched, the more surprised I was at the conclusions that emerged. I wanted to be sure the clarity of my hypothesis made sense. *Survival Quest* is my personal exploration of how to survive the game of life and how to go forward, continuing to challenge mortality.

Along my journey, my life and landscape have shifted, and I have uncovered my own brand of spirituality. I live in the moment whenever possible. Each day is filled with love, which changes how I approach and view situations.

My past is my past, but my future will reveal its unique challenges. I wish to live a full life to the bitter end, encountering strife and peril in order to endure and thrive with a greater reward, despite adversity and dangerous circumstances.

Sharing creativity through my books and photography, I hope to positively influence others, while suggesting ways to contribute to their growth and safety, so they will receive joy and a resulting peace. Because a lot of these stories revolve around the psychology of emotion, my background in psychology and articles written in that realm have assisted my search.

I will always keep striving, driven to overcome. If not risking, life is not full.

The survivor gets to tell the story.
from Nancy Werlin's novel,
The Rules of Survival

1

Up a Creek Without a Paddle

~

I have chosen to begin my book with this story about my own relationship, my will to live, and conquering fear. Our experiences could have been deadly if we had made wrong decisions.

This trip is what got me thinking about survival.

~

I LOVE TO TAKE ON SOMETHING UNUSUAL that stretches my abilities physically and mentally, puts me on the edge of being safe, and allows me to explore and prove I can adapt to unforeseen occurrences with confidence. How can I handle each new difficult situation? Challenges train you to quickly react to the things you encounter in your daily life and find solutions.

I found just such a challenge years ago, when I was married and traveling the Inside Passage of Alaska on a cruise with my husband and daughter. As we sat in our luxurious, warm cabin, looking out the window, we saw a couple kayaking among icebergs in the frigid water. They landed on a small, gray rock protruding from the water, dragged their boat ashore, and set up camp, completely alone for the night.

Why would they want to do that, or be able to do that? For years I thought on this.

Twenty-five years, to be exact. Now divorced and dating a daring fellow named Michael, I proposed that we explore Alaska's Glacier Bay. I had a special mission for the trip — to paddle the glacier-cold water, with its unforgiving environment, and re-create what I saw on that past trip. My partner agreed to complete my dream. My original vision of a few hours paddling paled with what we were tackling.

We traveled through the Inside Passage on the ferry MV *Baranoff*, with our tent duct-taped to the windy fourth-floor deck. It was an unusual camping venture, different than the many we'd shared on land, but we were rewarded with lots of wildlife sightings. We were one with our environment and each other, sharing life.

After arriving in Juneau, we flew on a bush plane to Gustavo Bay and regrouped. We were preparing to complete the goal we'd both envisioned, but first, we needed to register for a camping permit and view a mandatory orientation video, which was rather alarming.

The film talked about all the things you can die from. There was the biggest threat, hypothermia, and also getting lost, bears, and additional dangers.

We arrived in Glacier Bay, set up camp for the night, and watched numerous bears roaming near our campsite. Undeterred, we made our five o'clock orientation at the kayak rental company.

We learned to read topographical and tide maps. The tides would move in and out of the bay every twelve hours, they told us, and would either make our paddling easier or impossible, going from one inlet to another. If we misjudged the timing, we could find ourselves grounded in muck until the next tide arrived. Our only solution would be an arduous portage—if that was even possible.

It was imperative to understand everything if we were going to make our one-day window for a pickup a week later to return us to Gustavo Bay. Michael and I struggled as the reality of the dangers registered. We asked lots of questions, knowing we could, as always, rely on one another for more than we individually understood.

After the lesson, we were fitted with our splash gear, boots, life vests, kayak, and paddles. The paddles were broken into two pieces, with a male and female end, and we practiced joining them together and setting the angle of our blades.

The forecast for the week was rain and wind.

We boarded our drop-off boat the next morning, and enjoyed six hours of touring the bay before we reached our kayak launching point in Blue Mouse Cove. It was an astounding trip. Our guide pointed out the wildlife and explained how the icebergs we saw were just a fraction of what lay below the gray-blue surface. An iceberg could reverse direction at a second's notice, submerging a boat.

As we approached "our" bay, my stomach tightened. This was it. We would be completely on our own in the cold, nasty environment. No houses, boats, businesses, or park stations with rangers. *No cappuccino.*

The forecast was right. It rained torrents of frigid water, falling in sheets from black clouds as we got off the boat at 2:30 that afternoon. A group of eight young park workers disembarked with us. They would take a different route on a three-day excursion.

Our gear was thrown ashore first, and then we dropped our kayaks into the water and pushed the brightly colored boats toward land. We were knee-deep in the chilly water, working quickly. Michael and I hurriedly checked that we had all our bags and moved everything up to the rocky coastline as the largest tide gain in the Northern

Hemisphere surged toward us, two feet every fifteen minutes. The drop-off boat departed immediately to maintain its schedule.

Unloading from MV Baranoff for our paddle.

We ran around, re-inspecting our things as we packed our kayak. The last items we reached for were our paddles, just as the large group completed their loading and headed out on the water.

Alone on the beachfront, Michael held up our four paddle pieces and screamed incredulously.

"We have three female fittings and only one male!"

We could only fashion one complete paddle for our two-person boat.

It wasn't anger I heard in his voice, but disappointment and maybe fear. I, however, was furious that the rental company had sent us to this type of location, endangering our lives, without properly checking our gear.

We shouted to our fellow travelers, already disappearing across the waves. "Do you have an extra paddle?"

"No," they called back sympathetically. "Check with the Forest Service raft floating across the bay. They have a radio connected to the Gustavo Bay Lodge. We're sure they can help." Those were the last audible words we heard as they disappeared around the peninsula, heading north.

Water dripped from our chins as we looked at each other, stunned. We had no way to communicate with the outside world. We knew that we were not scheduled to see another soul for a week. We were completely on our own in a remote, stormy area, and we'd been instructed to not to stay where we were because of the bears. Camping on this rocky outcrop was "off limits."

We looked at the bay, each thinking that maybe we could take turns and paddle across it to one of the finger inlets we'd planned to explore, and then camp for the week there. Reading each other's minds, we both said out loud, "We can't!" Even if we were experienced kayakers, one set of oars wouldn't make headway against this tide, and we might tip in the choppy water. The orientation instructors had warned us that death would follow within minutes if we submerged in the frigid temps.

"We're fucked!" Michael screamed.

The only thing to do was to try to paddle around the cove, staying as close to shore as possible, and get to the Forest Service raft for help.

We both got in the boat, a large feat in itself as we had only practiced once back at the camp. We didn't tip it over, and we smoothly fit our tight Neoprene spray skirts around us and launched into the raging water. Michael took the full paddle and provided the power strokes and navigation. I attempted to help with my half of a paddle, moving it from one side to the other. The balance was tricky. If I left my paddle in the water for a second too long, the current almost pulled it from my hands, tipping us toward the water's edge.

We rocked from side to side at first, but soon found a rhythm. The wind blew our craft, and the rudder didn't work because Michael had unknowingly stuffed bags in the bowels of our boat up against the working ropes, disabling it.

Finally, we approached the Forest Service raft, which had a small deck built around a floating room. I clung to the jagged metal side, painfully holding the boat as steady as possible, while Michael pulled himself three feet up to the deck level.

He knocked, but to our dismay there was no one there. I shouted above the wind, "Try the door and see what's inside." It was open, and he returned shortly with good news. "There's a CB radio, and I'm going to try to call for help and ask someone to bring us a paddle tomorrow."

Michael had never used a CB radio before. After twenty minutes, I could hear him shouting, "We have an emergency," and then escalating it to "Mayday! Mayday!" (That was a bit extreme, I thought.) He could hear other voices, but they couldn't hear him.

When he still had no response, Michael helped me out of the boat, and we entered the shelter. There was a large

sign on the door that said "NO ENTRANCE BY UNAUTHOR-
IZED PERSONS. PARK PROPERTY, UNDER PENALTY OF LAW,
ORDINANCE ... "

We surveyed our situation again. It was warmer inside,
although there was no heat turned on to counter the
30-degree temperature. And it was dry. There was a bunk
bed with a sleeping bag and pillow laid neatly on it, a
stove, a few tools, playing cards, matches, lots of books,
battery-operated lights, and even a wall heater. Outside
on the deck there was water in refillable tanks labeled
"unpurified."

On the floor were two sets of slippers that appeared to
have never been used. I thought it wasn't bad, especially
as we watched the wind-driven rain pelt the windows,
and the platform rocked back and forth.

Exploring further, behind a curtain we found food:
pasta, spices and herbs, tea, and even cake mix. Oh, we
could survive here for a bit. But Michael said, "We won't
use the heat, lights, water, or food. We're not supposed to
be here."

I argued it was an emergency.

We waited. The afternoon wore on, and there was no
sign of a human. It was getting darker and colder. I started
to shiver. We decided to stay the night and unloaded most
of our things from the kayak, worried that it could tip
in the storm or float away. Besides, I wanted something
warm for dinner, and to put on more clothes.

It wasn't easy to lift up a rain-filled, gear-laden boat.
We turned it over on the deck to drain. Soaked again, we
went inside and changed clothes for the third time. My

shivering increased, and I begged Michael to turn the heat on for ten minutes to take the chill off. He was adamant. "No. We aren't supposed to be here."

We used our propane to cook our own dried food, and hung our wet clothes from the rafters. We played cards while waiting for the occupant to return. Our Jambalaya Mix (I counted about five slim slices of meat) was not bad, considering the circumstances.

We studied our maps and tidal sheets, and tried to formulate a plan for the next day as the storm's intensity picked up and we rocked violently side to side.

Hours later, in bed with the extra sleeping bag acting as a second blanket, I finally drifted off. But it was still the middle of the night when I felt Michael shaking me awake. "Sally, something is very wrong." He had been awake for hours, feeling like our raft was changing directions, turning in circles even though it shouldn't move. He finally went outside and found that one of the two heavy anchor chains that held the raft in place must have come unhooked.

With the storm still raging, Michael hypothesized that the other tether could give way during the night, and we might drift out of the cove into the more threatening water of the bay.

Alarmed, I was now fully awake. With the winds blowing fifteen to twenty miles per hour and wave swells of three to four feet, could the raft flip? We'd be trapped in a watery death, confined in this box at the water's floor.

I was now pacing with Michael. We had no solutions, but we stayed awake, waiting for daylight when we knew we would have to leave.

At dawn, fortified by a cup of tea and a PowerBar, things seemed better. We came up with opposing plans. I wanted to continue around the bay, staying near shore but finishing the trip. This plan depended on hitting the right tide for the passage to open. I thought the window of opportunity to leave was within the next two hours, but I was surely not a tidal expert.

Michael wanted to paddle directly to the tip of the peninsula, stand on the outcrop, and wave to attract any passing boat. I felt this location would be miles away from the boats that came by every few days, and we'd be in the elements.

Then we spotted a sailboat anchored across our cove. We guessed it was two miles away. Michael wanted to paddle across to their craft and ask them to call for help. I was reluctant to leave, giving up on what had been my goal for so long. I felt we could survive by paddling near shore to the inlets, camping, and enjoying that experience until the pickup boat arrived.

I finally acquiesced to Michael's plea to call it quits. I had never seen him so unsure, so unconfident. He was a master whitewater rafter of rivers, taking risks in that sport. But this was different; he was instead in a kayak and was out of his element.

I realized my own strength at that moment, but we were a team. I'd have to respect his wishes. It was a crushing blow to me, but it wasn't fair to ask him to risk his life.

The kayak was difficult to pack. We lowered it into the water and then dropped all our gear into the various crannies, while trying to keep the water out of our seating area so our boat wouldn't fill and sink.

Once again, our craft made a comical zigzag across the water with our lopsided paddling arrangement, but we made headway until we could see the occupants of the small craft laughing and enjoying their morning coffee. We were relieved, but soon they were pulling up anchor and starting to move.

Michael and I were both in a panic. The would-be saviors were abandoning our effort to be saved. We increased our speed, straightening our boat's trajectory. "Faster!" Michael screamed, and I put all my force behind my one lonely paddle. Where my strength came from, I don't know to this day.

They were now a distance from shore. We adjusted our point and attempted to follow them, at least keeping up with their forward movement. We frantically waved and shouted, but they didn't notice.

We persisted, and at last the woman on the sailboat, whose name I later learned was Beth, glanced back to where they had anchored and saw two crazy people in a kayak. On board with the engine running, she couldn't make out what we were yelling, but she realized by our actions that it must be important. She told her husband, Bill, to cut the engine, and we finally caught up to their craft.

We described our plight, and it wasn't long before this generous couple was helping us load our craft and gear onto their sailboat. They opened their cooler, passed out bottles of beer, and we finally relaxed. Bill and Beth doubled back on their own course to return us to the Glacier Bay Lodge, six hours away.

Reveling in our safety, we exchanged stories of our adventures. Bill and Beth had met while working at a restaurant and, for months, plotted their escape from the mundane world. Their dream was to sail to various parts of the world and host tourists on their boat.

But first, they needed a boat. Each paycheck went into the boat fund until they found this boat, which looked like a good deal. With no sailing experience, they had no idea how to gauge issues and potential repair costs. This was their first cruise in Alaska, and it had broken down three times already, costing them months of time and expense, sitting in ports and trying to get parts to this remote part of the world.

They were risk takers, though, and they just laughed at their situation as their funds diminished. They'd make it, just as Michael and I would. I could see the determination in their eyes.

2

White Wilderness
Expedition

Larry Difani packing into the Sierras.

＊

Michael and I purposefully took on risks, and were almost overwhelmed with fear. Larry, the mountain man, had no idea what he was taking on as he planned his short foray at season's end. He had three important assets waiting at home for his return.

＊

A farmer and developer in California's Central San Joaquin Valley for thirty years, Larry Difani has always spent his summers packing into the Emigrant Wilderness of the Sierras. He founded Difani's Backcountry Manufacturing, which sells pack equipment to customers all over the world. He is an active member of the Backcountry Horsemen, creating their Wilderness Rider Program, serving as State Education Chair, and cofounding the Mid Valley Unit. He has also served as president and master of Leave No Trace, and volunteered for a number of other organizations with a strong commitment to preserving our wilderness. Larry continues his summer pack trips into the wilderness he loves.

IT WAS SUMMER'S END, WITH JUST A NIP of frost during the early morning signaling a change around the corner, the precursor of new beginnings. With fall approaching, it was a bit late to take on another trip. It would be just a week or so into the Sierra wilderness, but you never knew when winter would show its face. Larry's wife reasoned that surely it wouldn't come this early, not with all these warm days they'd enjoyed together.

Wrong.

Larry inspected his stock for this trip—his favorite horse, Sunny, and the three mules that always worked well together. He put the dominant mule at the end of his pack string so that, if it kicked, the others wouldn't feel its hooves. Mules have better instincts for self-preservation than horses, rarely panicking or injuring themselves or their rider, so he weighted his string with mules. He rationalized the trip, saying that they needed training in the mountain passes.

Larry had been an adventurer all his adult life, moving to the edge of risk in business as well as the elements in backcountry trips. He was restless, hating to leave his family but ready for his yearly venture. With the peaches delivered and processed, he was free from obligations on the ranch; the check in the bank earned him time to roam his beloved mountains. His family understood. They were always anxious about his solitary travels, but knew his need for one more.

He'd had a disaster on a trail a few years before. He had taken his baby girls and wife on just the sort of trip he was about to take. The pack stock had been carefully secured with a pigtail (a loop of quarter-inch manila rope tied into a rigging that runs from the upper cinch ring on each side of the stock, which will break if the animals get in a jam). As he pushed his pack on a narrow, rocky trail, his family dismounted and walked ahead. What caused them, at this precise moment, to lower their bodies from their ride? Whatever it was, it saved their lives.

Larry heard a clash of hooves , saw chocolate-colored dust kicked into the blue sky, heard crunching slate, and then a wheel of animals rolled over the cliff, still connected, falling in pinwheel turns. The pigtail rope did not release.

What had happened? Was there a snake on the trail that had spooked the animals?

The horses fell down the steep, rocky mountainside, slicing flesh as they toppled to the lake below. Larry and his wife looked over the edge and witnessed struggling animals, still attached to each other and desperately attempting to swim in the water below. Larry's mind raced; if he did not act immediately, he would lose them all—including his favorite, Freddie.

He could see Freddie sinking, fighting to surface, and then submerging once again. Larry grabbed his knife, took a literal leap of faith, and within seconds was in the clear lake with his livestock as they thrashed for their lives.

With a deep breath, he dove under the water, cutting the thick rope that bound each animal. On his final surface, he looked for Freddie. His backcountry friend never appeared.

Due to Larry's quick action, he did recover the remainder of his stock, but he mourned the mule that was more than stock to him. Freddie had been his companion for many years of traveling. His pack leader. The family was grateful to return home — safe.

For this year's trip, Larry's wife lovingly helped him pack the staples, along with special treats — steak, wine, brandy, and candy. The good stuff.

The pack team moved forward on the perfect autumn day, as leaves relinquished their green and dressed in yellows and oranges. It was beautiful and warm as Larry kissed his wife's ivory cheeks, her blond locks framing her face as they shared one last embrace. He lovingly picked up each young child and cherished her in his arms as he promised he'd return soon. He would soon be back in his comfortable home, with his wife cooking wonderful gourmet meals, pampering him, and with a child on each leg as he played with them and read nighttime stories by the flames of a roaring fire.

It was a much longer trip than he expected.

Larry arrived in the backwoods with his stock and moved forward with anticipation. How excited he was to be in the wild!

Life was good.

He had saddled, laden Decker Pack Saddles with bags of supplies, and at first he moved forward through warm temperatures. Climbing in elevation, the air began to cool, as expected. Larry wondered if he should add a layer over his plaid wool shirt. No, he would keep moving upward, navigating the switchbacks. He had a schedule for his trip and a return date to maintain.

It was getting dark; he found a perfect site and struck camp. The next day, he climbed again, moving from five thousand feet toward the mountaintop four thousand feet higher. He followed a narrow, winding path as he hugged the clouds. With the thought of a possible fall never far from his mind, he encouraged his stock to lean toward the vertical rock on one side as they climbed up the steep grade.

Trained by their master, each mule obeyed his urging. His insistent messages encouraged his stock to move forward, upward, over the slippery rocks and through the increasing cold that Larry did not notice as he focused on the night's destination.

As evening approached, Larry arrived at a plausible campsite. On first inspection he knew it wasn't perfect, but it was the best he could find. He released his stock to graze down below as he set up camp.

Soon Larry saw that his campsite was far from ideal. He surveyed the site, alarmed, as his intuition and previous experience told him that this was one of the worst situations imaginable. A valley swept before him, funneling wind directly to his chosen spot. Looking to the left, he saw a huge pile of rocks, presumably built by previous travelers for protection from the gusts that lashed across this exposed area.

He knew he should not stay, but with night approaching, it was too late to move.

As he tried to relax, he noticed his head mule, Molly, leading the stock back out the way they had arrived. Larry didn't usually feel the need to use the hitch line to tie his stock up, preferring to leave them free to graze. They were normally very loyal to their master and wouldn't leave him stranded. But then they did.

He caught up with the animals, scolding the team he walked them back to the meadow. This happened three times, the stock whinnying in defiance each time. Something just was not right; he had an eerie feeling of impending disaster when he finally tied them in for the night.

Then it happened. The sky opened up, and rain poured forth. It was light at first, then driving as it whipped his tent. Another fall mountain storm, he thought. Then lightning struck. The bolts arched toward the unprotected camp on the mountaintop, and Larry realized his extreme exposure on the granite slab. He thought about the metal shoes on his team's hooves, the metal on his own camp gear, and the metal on all the exposed rocks around him. There was nowhere to run as the light show continued.

As the night cooled, the precipitation changed to beautiful white flakes of snow. Wind started beating his small canvas tent, soon laden with frozen moisture. It was like a huge winter snowstorm, and it was upon him.

Larry huddled in his small two-person tent, his lantern lit for warmth, and swore as he thought about the larger four-person tent he normally would have loaded on his mules; it would have been much better, much more comfortable. He had brought four animals that could carry almost anything into this environment. But at this point, it no longer mattered. Here he was, and here he would stay.

That night, as the wind whipped the canvas, wisps of frigid air struggled to enter his enclosure. After a couple swigs of brandy, Larry slept like a babe and barely heard his stock whinny in the moonless dark outside.

When he woke, he tried to focus his mind on what he saw. It was nasty. Snowflakes continued to fall, and the wind picked up again with slashing force, telling all living beings that it was time to retreat. He checked his horse and mules; they were still hitched to the line and could not wander or get lost in what was now becoming a blanket of white. He returned quickly to his tent, and peeking out the flap he realized the gravity of his situation. The gods of the mountains were raging outside. It was a blizzard.

He was alone in the Sierras.

The brandy got him through the next three days, as Larry couldn't go anywhere in the whiteout, not even far enough to feed his stock. He relished the harshness of the experience, never feeling fearful. He never panicked, but decided to wait out the storm.

As time passed, though, Larry knew his stock had not had food for days. The storm wasn't diminishing, but he needed to move ahead or all five of them would soon be dead.

At morning light, he saddled his stock and packed up camp. He made one major mistake, letting his snow-laden tarp get close to his body while he folded it. The snow permeated his clothes, leaving his shirt and pants wet. Yet somehow he started down the path, barely able to see the next step of his horse's hooves on the narrow, rocky cliff. With faith, he depended and trusted Sunny to find the right footing, knowing that the next movement forward might mean a misstep and death, as they were all toggled together.

As they made their way down the trail, cold, damp snow forced into the fibers of Larry's clothes. Soon he was shaking uncontrollably. Wet and saturated, he recognized, as a mountain man would, hypothermia. He was miles from his destination, and his body temperature was rapidly dropping.

He needed to act, or his life would be lost. Larry drew from his experience from past trips, survival courses, and books. He knew it is possible to survive an average of three weeks without food, less without water, but hypothermia requires immediate action. Within the first forty-eight hours, cold kills. People lose their logic, and minds fill with a world of wishes, not reality. This can be deadly.

Larry stopped his animals on a narrow precipice, got off, and with luck did not join the falling rocks that crashed down the steep terrain. Reaching in a pannier, he recovered a dry fleece sweatshirt. He quickly stripped to bare flesh as the sleet pelted his body, dropped his drenched garments, and encased his torso with heat. A new energy brought color to his blue skin.

The shaking stopped. His body knew the comfort of a warm, dry layer.

They went onward in the still-attacking snow. Larry did not know his path—maybe forward, maybe down, maybe this was not the direction. All of his training and experience told him to stay on the higher trail, as the snow in the lower elevation paths could hide major hazards of rocks or fallen tree branches that could entrap them. But with his animals' hooves slicing against rock, slipping on snow with little control, Larry moved forward with a mission. He would go down to the bottom of the valley, even though he risked the possibility of no wife, no family, and no life. Assured he would return safe, he continued.

The stock slid, and everything stopped. Recovering, never panicking, Larry acknowledged he was alive for the moment and intently focused his efforts on moving forward.

He rode toward the origin of this trip—his truck—and thought about warmth and being dry. He passed a Yosemite Park sign that he remembered from when he started out. He must be on the right trail, though now he could barely see the letters under the snow.

An hour later, he wasn't so sure. Could he have made a wrong turn, lost his trail?

Again he stopped. The cold froze his body to the bone. Calmly, he reassessed his situation, turned, and retraced his steps upward until he reached the familiar sign. He did this three times, doubting his path, misjudging distances in the snow.

His stock were exhausted; he was exhausted. Sunny collapsed. She was giving her all for her master, but she was not as strong as the mules. Larry tried to coax her up.

Nothing happened. This horse was done. Yet he could not leave her to die. He picked up a stick and did what was abhorrent to him, hitting his beloved horse. She rose and continued.

There was not much time left before the dark, cold night, and no place to erect camp on this rocky, narrow path as the snow continued to bombard them.

Assessing his situation, he focused on what he must do next. If he was to have any chance of survival, he needed to continue downward. He may be on the wrong trail and die, but if he did not move forward, he most surely would.

With determination and confidence, Larry kicked his horse's barrel side, wet with snow, and progressed forward. They were all exhausted and just about spent, and he questioned how he would end this journey alive.

Then Larry experienced what he called a "miracle" of intervention, a surprising word coming from a non-spiritual person. A sliver of light cut through an opening in the clouds above him for mere seconds, focusing like a prism on the narrow valley below. It showed his path home, and then it was gone.

Angels? God? A divine spirit? It didn't matter; Larry knew his direction to safety. With renewed energy, he picked up speed. He trusted his stock to guide them back. They seemed to feel his excitement, his renewed confidence, and his drive to overcome. A short hour later, he found himself safe at the valley floor, contemplating what had just happened.

Larry came home a slightly different man, with a new belief that there are things that humans can't explain, yet they shape our destiny. He did not talk to anyone for a long time about what had occurred, but it influenced his life going forward.

Why had he made it off the mountain? His assets that helped conquer this challenge were seemingly simple ones—his persistence, his strong desire to return to a family he loved, his drive to overcome, his experience with risk in his daily living, and his ability to find solutions to successfully mounting challenges.

3

Lost in the Canadian Woods

～

Larry found internal strength and depended on his intuition, but was surprised at the guidance he received from outside our worldly realm. It moved me to listen to him telling the story and see his emotion. Going forward, I will explore what part spirituality plays in crises.

I often go it alone into the wilderness. Oh, not on Larry's scale. It's on a Sally scale. But, like Larry, I found a savior I didn't expect. I'm a pretty confident woman, so I was surprised what an impact this event had on me.

～

IN CANADA, NEAR THE SMALL TOWN OF Golden and just west of Lake Louise in Alberta, I was on one more of my wandering escapes, this time with my beloved dog, Tasha. I'd raised her from a pup, and she had been my companion for eight years; we enjoyed a uniquely close bond. While I usually traveled alone, I was happy to share my experiences with my Lab/rottweiler mix.

We settled into a rented cabin in the mountains, forty miles outside of town. It was a cedar bungalow, cozy with French lace drapes, accents of cherry red, and a knockout view of the mountains beyond. I loaded fir logs into the fireplace and was pleased to get the fire going. I never know if the wood where I stay will be green or aged, but these were dry. I relaxed, drained from the day's drive.

The owner knocked on the door and suggested I take a walk with my companion. Oh, when Tasha heard the word "walk," it could not be ignored.

The fall temperatures were cooling, the leaves were golden orange, and after just arriving from the drive, I hesitated. The man assured me. "You will not have a problem walking up the mountain alone. You have a dog. Yes, there is snow, but it's not deep, the trail is well marked, and you can be home before dark."

It was three o'clock, and sunset was two hours away.

I was so warm, so relaxed, I wanted to nix the thing and read on the couch. But my dog, who clearly had heard the word "walk," had her own opinion. I squeezed into my old, worn, comfortable hiking boots. Looking at the single inch of snow on the ground and the sun warming the crisp air, I put on a light jacket. I attached a leash to Tasha, who had never listened to me, even as a pup. She was a defiant alpha who needed to be tethered. She was, as I am, untrainable.

We set out, the dog pulling so that I could barely hold her. Excited, she ran in every direction, sniffing the new scents of this place. As we climbed, the snow level increased. It was exhilarating in the chilly air. We were in our environment.

The trail was well marked until we came to a fork in the road. The right led down. That could not be correct. The owner had said the trail was clearly marked, so we continued up. The snow deepened, and I noticed there were no more flag markers. Had we made the wrong move? Should we have turned right?

I stopped, concentrating on the correct direction. The chill in the air was increasing, and the sun was lowering. I was now fully aware, not thinking about how pretty the trees and snow were. I needed to make an immediate decision.

We retraced our steps downward, and this time I saw the flag marking the downhill path we hadn't taken. Maybe this was our best path home to the cozy cabin. It dropped steeply, so at least that was positive.

The sun was starting to set. I was getting cold and cursed that I had not brought a warmer jacket, hat, and gloves for what I thought would be a quick stroll. Tasha and I had to fight low tree limbs and slippery muck below the snow melt, the result of the day's warm sunshine.

Another fork. Right or left? There were no markings.

I swore at the man. How could he encourage a lone woman to take on the trail at this late hour?

I started to question myself. Should we retrace our steps again, go back to the main trail? I turned to go uphill, but it was late, and that would surely take too long. And actually, after all the turns we had taken, I wasn't sure I could find it.

I had no flashlight. Tasha whimpered and wanted to go up, but I was sure—well, again, kind of sure—that down would be faster. Soon the small trees in the pathway entangled us. What had seemed like a path was now nothing. Twisting and turning, I was making my own path by intuition and the way my dog was pulling.

We came to a clearing. I was a bit frantic about spending the night out here with whatever wild animals must be nearby. The temps would drop below freezing, and we had no food, no matches, and no warm clothes. My dog was panting, her golden eyes making contact with mine.

I dropped to a log to compose myself. Aren't you supposed to stay in one place and not wander when you're lost, waiting until someone finds you? But who'd be looking for us in the wilderness? I was cold, I was hungry, and I was tired.

I couldn't make a fire to warm us, so I decided I'd better figure out how we were going to survive with the wild creatures I was sure were now watching us. There must be grizzly bears, since this was a protected area for them. Maybe mountain lions, wolves … oh, my imagination was running rampant.

So I made a plan. I would find a stick, dig a hole in the frozen soil (oh, sure), and cover our cuddling bodies with fir branches. Tasha was almost a hundred pounds and she always kept me warm when we camped, but that was in a tent. We'd be a strange twosome out here. I'd put a stick near our heads to ward off animal attacks.

Tasha was not happy sitting at my feet. She seemed to feel my distress as she nuzzled me and whined. She was not content to be here in the cold forest. Maybe she, too, was thinking about our warm fire in the cabin. This is not where we should be in the dark.

At last she got up and started tugging, with all her strength, on her leash. She pulled me up to my feet, and we set off running down the hill with a vengeance, branches lashing and attacking our bodies. Oh goodness, I always had a hard time controlling her.

But within minutes of running, tripping over the pathless snow, I stopped and screamed.

I saw the road we had been searching for. Tasha had saved us. (How, I always have wondered?)

That night I shared part of my steak with my rescuer and vowed never to strike out on a hike without warm clothes, a bit of food and water, a knife, a small first aid kit, and matches. In the years since, I've never again forgotten these things. But, my most important, lifesaving tool was my dog. Tasha is no longer my constant companion, so I'm also more cautious about hiking alone, always letting someone know where I'm going and for how long.

Being lost your mind fools you and you lose yourself. It is like having no self. *It's someone else in this situation, surely not you.* You can feel confused, claustrophobic, panicky, and waste energy moving around to find your way.

There have been studies of basic human needs. One of the first is the need for a mother's gaze; it makes a connection for the baby. Without that, the baby might not progress in normal development, and can even die. Being lost is similar. In a basic state, being lost creates a loss of connection, and in the resulting terror, rational thinking is thrown aside, leaving confusion.

When you're first lost, you are not sure what you see or what you want to see. You admit being lost and feel frantic, but have no plan. If you devise a strategy, it is often based on what you want to see, and you become less rational as you fail and run out of energy. Finally, you trust you can find your way out, admit to yourself no one will come to your rescue, and you take responsibility by devising a new, more rational plan.

I went through many of these phases. Tasha kept me focused, and wouldn't let me rest until we were back in the cabin. She felt night would soon be upon us, she smelled the animals, and she knew her master was stressed.

I have traveled all over the world by myself, but this evening of being lost was one of my most terrifying experiences.

4

Free-Falling Lane

Lane Lamoreaux dressed for action as a smokejumper.

People come into our lives for a reason, so it is important to always be open to what's new.

I learned from my experience of being lost in the woods that maybe, just maybe, I cannot always be in control. I also learned to defer to another's direction for rescue, even if it is not a human.

Searching for answers about what makes a survivor, I was in the perfect place to meet Lane, who moved my understanding forward by quantum leaps. He showed me the whys and hows, and was I lucky I'd dropped into this particular place on this day.

What did Lane do right?

Lane is a smokejumper for the U.S. Forest Service, and he spends six months a year battling wildfires across the country. Their base is just a couple of miles from my home in McCall, Idaho, and I often pause as I drive home from my errands to watch this fit team train on the canopy wires or run miles in the mountains. They parachute in to battle these disasters, acting decisively while remaining calm, always considering safety first. Lane taught English in Thailand and has a master's degree from Northern Arizona University's College of Education. He is currently rated as an Advanced Pilot, Tandem T-1, and a Basic and Paraglide Instructor.

I MET LANE AT A LOCAL COFFEEHOUSE IN our small Idaho town. Looking up from my computer to take in the new snowfall on the white-capped lake outside the window, surrounded by majestic mountains, I dreamt of launching my Advanced Elements kayak for the last time of the season.

He caught my eye as he looked up from his Nikon camera, which he'd aimed at the canning jars lining the shelves of the rustic restaurant. He moved closer to his subject just as I do, trying to find that perfect composition for an abstract photograph. I immediately related to what he was discovering through his lens. It would be a macro view of his encounter—the perfect relationship between shapes and colors, but probably not a recognizable object, to elicit an emotion from the viewer.

I crossed the uneven wood floor, focused like an insect trying to capture a similar being in her web. I wanted to meet this guy.

We spoke about our photo passions and what he and I were currently working on. I noticed his cane and glanced down to his injured leg. I cautiously asked what had happened, and without hesitation he shared his story with a perfect stranger. Lane's injury occurred during the "off season" from his smokejumper's job, when he decided to paraglide in California just for the fun of it.

While he was soaring through the sky, an unexpected, unusual shift of downhill current grabbed his glider and thrust it toward the earth at accelerating speed, leaving Lane with little control of his craft. His parachute refused to open, and he crashed to the earth below. Only then did his reserve chute open, dragging his body an additional sixty feet over nearby boulders, ripping and tearing his flesh and soul.

Luckily, his paragliding partner, Scott, saw what happened. Within ninety seconds he was by Lane's side and immediately radioed for an emergency air rescue.

A pilot who happened to be in the vicinity had his radio on and heard Scott's message. He relayed the request for the emergency air rescue six miles beyond Scott's communication range. Without this assistance, the recovery team may not have arrived in time to save Lane's life.

It was difficult terrain to access the patient. Yet in just thirty minutes, a Cal Fire heavy Huey chopper arrived. It rendezvoused with paramedics in a Mercy 3 aircraft for transport to Riverside County Regional Medical Trauma Services.

Lane regained consciousness in the swirl of dust, but remained calm as he assessed his injuries and what his path forward would be. He felt no pain for the first two minutes. He looked down at his leg, which was at a right angle to his body, reached down, and made an adjustment to straighten it—in essence, breaking it back into alignment. Doctors said later that this saved his leg from much further trauma.

You're not supposed to survive one-hundred-foot falls that incur a traumatic brain injury and push your femur and pelvis into your ribs, lacerating the organs in their path, but Lane did.

One hour after the accident, with multiple agencies participating in the speedy response, Lane was in a full-service hospital. His blood pressure was 86/50, his respiratory rate 31 and shallow, his skin cold and pale, and he registered a 6 on the coma scale. Medical records show his state as anxious and confused, with his heartbeat at a high level of 120–140 and blood loss at 1,500–2,000 milliliters. He was in phase III or IV, which is identified as *deceased* according to all measurements—but, he was still, miraculously, alive.

There were ten professionals from the Trauma Team working on Lane. Within just twelve minutes of his arrival, he was stabilized. But when he received a new transfusion, his blood pressure plummeted to 56/26.

Almost two hours into the ordeal, the doctors lost Lane's pulse and started CPR. He was rushed into surgery and given massive blood transfusions. Four hours of surgery followed.

The first twelve hours are critical for survival. Lane continued to receive substantial blood transfusions, and he stabilized by the next day. He remained under Riverside's care for forty days, and he was in a coma most of the time. Friends visited him, including many from his smokejumper crew. Amazingly, he remembers each visit, despite his altered state. Their support and love must have had a positive effect on his fight to live.

When he surfaced and faced our living world, the hospital released him to an Arizona ICU. Lane's friends continued to rally during his recovery, getting the word out and creating a fund to help pay his medical expenses. One of their requests was to send positive energy his way. They talked about Lane's resilience, both mental and physical.

In just a few short months Lane moved forward from the place where his doctors declared he would never walk again and became the man I was talking to. Lane was now paralyzed in one leg from the knee down, and his peripheral vision in one eye was limited. Yet standing with the aid of a cane, he described his next adventure to Thailand, where, he said, "the gentle people live." He had enjoyed previous visits, and he longed to return. Something was driving him forward.

I searched for the reasons Lane struggled to recover and succeeded. What I found was surprising at first, until, during my book research, I found evidence that affirmed how many of his attributes helped his survival and recovery.

Lane had tremendous support from family and friends, who prayed for him. He had a positive mental attitude. After his injury, he fought to move forward and he enthusiastically embraced life.

Lane has always challenged himself, but he also made safety a high priority in the way that he tackled risky pursuits. He knew how to act decisively. He stayed calm in the face of adversity, looked death in the face, and found something wondrous and inspiring in his coma state. Recovering, he had resilience, both mental and physical, against all of the odds stacked against him.

Lane is a tough guy, a bright spirit, and a fighter with an indomitable will to live. These are some of the qualities of a survivor.

In November 2013, one year after his accident, he was invited to the Riverside County Regional Annual Trauma Conference for a presentation. It was a memorable day for Lane, as well as the ICU nurses and audience in the room. The speaker explained the time progression from when Riverside Hospital received the call of a downed paraglider to Lane's release from the hospital. He explained that the medical staff never expected him to walk. And then, to everyone's surprise, the patient actually walked on stage and cordially accepted a plaque with the inscription:

In honor of your will to survive
Lane Lamoreaux
Your Riverside Medical Center Family

When I asked Lane why he felt he survived when others die from similar injuries, this is what he said:

Why did I survive? I think a big part of it has been all the endeavors I've chosen to take on through my life. I was pretty much an underdog in everything I did. I showed up on the football field as the thinnest, least coor-

dinated guy out there, but by midseason I was hailed as
having a work ethic others could aspire toward. The same
thing happened when I joined the Marines, and again
when I was hired by the McCall Smokejumpers. Having
the odds stacked against me seems to be a familiar occur-
rence. I take pride in these circumstances as I impress oth-
ers by prevailing — including myself.

Lane's survival was a result of the undertakings he'd
chosen through his life and his devotion to doing a good
job. It was a pattern of defiance and excellence.

He also shared with me:

While I was in a coma, my body may have been asleep,
but my mind was as active as it's ever been. I synthesized
my surroundings with my imagination to create vivid and
at times lucid dreams. Most of the dreams were downright
terrifying! I was paranoid and believed the hospital staff
was putting me through several life-threatening scenarios
to see if I would make the right choice. The wrong choice
would result in death. They were all time-sensitive sce-
narios, like having the walls close in on me, tentatively
squeezing me to death, and being in a cave when it
became flooded, increasingly limiting the supply of air.
Crazy stuff.

He now feels that all this turmoil in his brain must
have had a positive effect on his fight to live. His cog-
nition and response process, even while in a coma, was
expressed and enhanced by the visual images he encoun-

tered and created. Before this occurrence, he had read a book on survival, and that, too, may have saved his life.

I could tell from the beginning of our conversation that Lane was a survivor. I'm not sure how, but after studying people my whole life, learning to be perceptive and use all my senses, I know who the lucky ones are. They're the people with guts.

A year and a half after we first met, I was surprised to see him back in the coffee shop where we first became friends. Instead of his cane, he was now on crutches.

A new story unfolded. Lane had made miraculous progress and had been proudly walking without the aid of his cane. A very physical guy, he wanted to get into the mountains and take his first hike. Luckily, he made the right decision and did not venture on the trail alone.

In July that year, it was dry and dusty. Lane and his friend had walked about a mile and a half when his walking stick slipped as he stepped on a rock, and his body twisted. Once again, his leg went in one direction, his body in the other. He heard a snap and crumbled to the earth. It was a small fall in comparison to his last disaster, but he immediately knew something was broken. It must be his damn leg.

After a call from his hiking partner, volunteers from the McCall Smokejumpers arrived, picked up their fallen friend, and carried him the long distance back up and down the mountain trail. Lane felt the excruciating pain of each jolt.

He was one lucky fellow to have friends and caring people surrounding and assisting in his rescues.

He went to the local hospital, where a talented doctor worked on his body. It was no normal procedure, as there was already so much metal patching Lane up from his previous fall, but the physician found an unusual path. He inserted yet one more piece of metal—this time a titanium rod that would hold his femur in place.

I met Lane just three weeks into his new recovery. He was out, employed, but I knew he must be dealing with agonizing pain. You just wouldn't know it to look at his smiling, demure face. He seemed so relaxed. Maybe there is more, something substantial that calls out to others, his enormously strong will to go forward yet one more time.

A miraculous will to conquer adversity.

Survival, in Lane's case, is partially due to his calm, analytical nature, his strong will to live, and the support of his friends and family. If you remain calm in crisis, rely on all you've learned to combat a particular situation and objectively look at the solutions and what action you should take, you will have made the first step to conquering.

5

The Fighter

⌁

*The following story has similar qualities to Lane's,
but with diverse ages and a completely different
environment — the land of illness and confinement.*

*How could two stories that seem so different share
the same striving to live and a similar outcome?*

*In life, we receive gifts that assist us, both emotionally
and physically, in surviving. Fighting death with a
strong desire to live greatly improves our chances
of survival. This story may have offered me the best
lessons for my future growth on so many levels, and
it will hopefully influence your survival, as well.*

⌁

WHEN DOES A PERSON RELINQUISH THE will to live and choose death instead?

In 2000, Mom had invasive surgery to remove her gallbladder, as well as other organs that were infected with gangrene, which almost ended her life. That was followed by numerous hospital trips to save a woman who seemed destined to meet her maker. Yet Mom fought these dangers with strength, bravery, and a positive attitude. She just wasn't ready to cash it all in.

Showing the same strength after Dad's death, she set out at the age of eighty to go it alone, learning how to maintain her home by doing her own repairs, holding it together financially, and bridging the chasm of loneliness. We built a bond by talking often, and I got to understand who my mother is. She always listens, and she makes me feel accepted and empowered. But most of all, we share our love.

Twelve years after that first medical emergency, we faced one more struggle.

I was opposed, most of my life, to showing any emotion. I carefully regulated myself to skirt events that would trigger either heartfelt sadness or elation. I was successful with that restraint. But one day, a particularly sad thing happened to me, and I relayed it to my boyfriend, Arthur, while we were standing in the middle of a gift shop. I looked up and saw tears welling in his eyes. He held me close for five minutes, and we both sobbed while customers walked around us. I learned about empathy from this man. (He also taught me about surrender ... but that is another story.)

I never expected to feel Mom's pain, or to care for someone who was dying. But when the call came, I remembered Arthur and what he taught me. Empathy can actually help you survive.

Mom could not eat and had no appetite. Her mouth was infected from a nine-month-old suture wound left from a tooth extraction. There was a horrible gap in her mouth that never healed. This was the beginning of her downward curve.

I drove across states to assess the situation. What followed was a roller coaster, with daily highs and lows of emotion. Early on, with the help of various websites, I suspected that I was seeing end-of-life symptoms. I shared this with my siblings and encountered their strong denials. Only I, ever present on the battlefront, saw the truth of her deteriorating condition.

Barely able to rise from a chair or couch, she ate little and slept incessantly. The light in her eyes diminished.

As time passed, Mom was in and out of the hospital, but she was still in the present. She was confined to a single bed in her den for eighteen months. One day, as light filtered through the partially drawn drapes from the patio, I realized we were alone. Gone, at least for a few hours, was the constant stream of paid caretakers who arranged her linens, adjusted her clothes, changed what needed to be changed. Her ever-present, caring husband, Hal, had also stepped out. Mom and Hal had been married eleven years, and I admired how he had so much compassion for his wife. Hal just wanted her there with him for one more day of their ninety-one-year lives.

She was amazingly focused, willing to continue on this path. Mom's defiance amazed me after all the trials of her illness. How could any human want to continue with the daily boredom of bed confinement and pain?

I felt slumber knocking against my exhausted body. I was struggling to ward off a virus while traveling, and I felt emotionally drained after dealing with family matters. I saw the empty shell I'd become.

On my last night of that visit to Mom's, Hal and I struggled to get her upstairs to bed where she slept each night. She gallantly moved against gravity, slowly shuffling her sneakers, which she always insisted on wearing in order to be properly dressed.

She could barely talk, but she communicated in other essential ways. Her sad, reluctant eyes still expressed emotion as her mouth fought to form words. I listened intently. My heart saddened, but I tried not to hint of my inner tears in her presence.

In the morning, I felt a ray of hope as I enjoyed two minutes of almost normal talk from Mom. Then the weakness set in again, and sadly I watched her realize it was one more day of the slide. A day of caregivers—a nurse, physical therapy, and special visitors—who would guide her toward (I needed to admit what was coming) death. Each time someone left, she closed her eyes and drifted to a place where she felt safe. She has a brilliant mind, and I thought it might be a blessing if it was dulled, but its complexity remained intact.

I returned home across the states. After a brief seven days in Idaho, Hal called again. "I need you here," he said.

Mom was exhausted from the doctor visits and being moved like a rag doll by caregivers who hurt her body. It was difficult to move 130 pounds, limp without muscle strength. Her eyes lost their sparkle, her skin paled, her feet became ice cubes to my touch, and her appetite disappeared. Her vision blurred with her life. It was just a friggin' pain to go on.

At home one night, Mom asserted herself and said she'd sleep downstairs in the den. She was just too tired to go up. Hal insisted on sleeping at her feet on the uncomfortable couch. The next day, he coaxed her to sleep in their bed upstairs again. He grinned, jumping up and down just like a child as he told her, "I promise I won't try to cover you up." (That always woke Mom.)

Mom was slipping. She was so much weaker than previous week. In adjacent chairs, with a dimpled smile, she announced to Hal, "We are almost touching toes." But the moment was robbed. Hal said, "What?" as he adjusted his almost useless, but very expensive, hearing aid. Her small mouth folded, no longer upturned, her delight of a close moment eluded.

Silent, each closed their eyes, lost in solitary worlds that drifted off.

Mom's cheerleaders—her caretakers—moved her forward as she stumbled. After they left, she cried in frustration to me. "It is my life. Let me go, let me die my way."

It was a shock, but I heard her. I was the only one capable of acknowledging her desire, the only supporter for the opposing team. I would continue to advocate *for her*. I'd be darn mad if someone made me live when I decided it to be my time to go, my peaceful passing, my glorious termination of suffering.

The next day I was sitting on a cold, navy seat in the emergency ward of the hospital, under the glare of fluorescent bulbs, as Mom drifted in and out of slumber. She was cold and pale; I think she was worried as they conducted tests to see why she'd fainted and threw up in the doctor's office. I held her frail, shaking body, and I told her I was there, that I always would be there. The nurse called 911, and we made the second ride to the hospital in seven days.

EKG, X-rays, blood tests, CAT scans, and urine work. Poke, poke, poke. An IV.

A rash emerged. Her white blood cell count was high for no apparent reason. To her frustration, I couldn't make out her feeble words as she moved listlessly in bed, clawing at the bedding, not able to find a comfortable position. She did not eat, drank little, and continued to show signs of impending death.

More pills appeared, these for nausea to treat her upset stomach. I asked if this would make her drowsy. Yes.

Goddamn the medical professionals who can't figure out the Dying with Grace game.

I watched as she drifted mercifully into her own best place. A sharp, alert mind shrouded in a decaying body.

An assistant took her pulse. "Eighty-seven," she told me when I asked.

Mom struggled to say something. I moved closer, put my ear to her lips, and she angrily whispered, "No. Eighty-nine." She was watching the monitor and caught this person's error. Oh my.

The next day, when I arrived in Mom's hospital room, I saw a shriveled, slumped woman, barely able to open her eyes to greet me.

She was tremendously drugged. Drugged on Metoprolol to regulate her heart, drugged on Benadryl to decrease the itching from the fire-red rash that covered her body, drugged on the pills to quiet her stomach. Drugged on drugs. There was no quality of life left in the attempts to improve her chances of survival.

I was done with modern medicine. I wished all those involved would go to hell. What were we doing to this bright lady? I called my brother and sister, describing the situation, pleading for us to request a stop of the worst offender, the Metoprolol medication for her heart. She should die on her own terms, coherent, not at the whim of the Hippocratic Oath.

The next day, I took the stark elevator to the third floor, rounded the corner, hoping there was still a body in the second bed of room 341. I was shocked.

A small, pink-haired lady sat up, alert and waiting for me. (Mom's hair had turned from gray to pink for some unknown reason.) She had survived the night, they had stopped her heart medicine and Benadryl, and she was talking almost perfectly. She proceeded to talk *all day,* with very little slurring. She had made a remarkable recovery.

I looked at the bottle of electrolytes constantly dripped into her vein and at the oxygen that replenished her body. "You are back," I exclaimed. She smiled and nodded.

Mom was pissed that she couldn't read the tempting menu in her hands because she didn't have her glasses. I ran to the car where I'd left them, propped them on her face, and she proceeded to order ten items. This was a woman who had not eaten more than a few bites and had no interest in food for months; now she hit the jackpot of food selections with boundless anticipation.

It was a good day for Mom and a very good day for her worried children.

But, the incessant rash was running rampant.

Her cardiologist arrived during the afternoon and explained that Mom just couldn't tolerate any more heart adjustment medicine; he had tried all of the medications in that family of drugs, but no more. I looked up at the handsome, gray-haired savior. He was stopping the medicinal attacks on her body. He explained clearly what this meant. There would be no more help to control a racing heartbeat. There would be no more zombie states, but possible death.

Death is a difficult concept for the elderly — or any person — to wrestle with. When is it enough to stop rescuing? How do you willingly give up your existence? Are you at peace with this? Have you done all you wish, lived your life to its fullest? What is the next one like?

The doctor, now concerned about the rash, prescribed steroid injections, which posed their own set of problems. When he remarked on the rash spreading to her face, she quipped, "You should see my bottom!" We all laughed, and he replied, "Well, certainly not while Hal's here." Despite her serious condition, Mom still retained a sense of humor.

As I was leaving that day, she said with a sparkle, "I just may make it." She sought to endure a bit longer. Despite wanting to cash it all in last week, now she wanted to go forward. And I knew that with a positive attitude, and intent to live, you can survive.

The next day was also good. Mom was spunky and more combative than she had been lately. I just loved her spirit. She asked if she could have eye surgery for her droopy eyelids. She was feeling on top of the world, with hope for the future.

She also fumed. "No doctor is helping me. This hospital is useless, and why am I here?" I heard her frustration and thought, why *is* she here?

The next morning, we spent wonderful time together. It was another day of her normal persona. We even got into one of our giggling fits, like the old days. Hal kept saying, "Don't laugh; you'll elevate your mom's blood pressure," but what a way to go. I had to leave the room three times to compose myself. Maybe it was our reprieve from the anxiety and fear.

Mid-morning, an assistant appeared with a dose of the dreaded Metoprolol. I asked her to check with the doctor. But when she returned, she handed Mom the pill and a glass of water. I never understood why, who prescribed the renewal of this drug. We knew what would follow.

I now wished for a clear death. Are more days beneficial? I could no longer judge.

Within days, she was transferred to a nursing home for "rehabilitation." If she didn't work on improving her physical state each day, soon would be her dismissal from the facility.

Hal and I filled out paperwork, and then joined Mom in her austere, two-person room, similar to her hospital digs. She was sitting on her bed, again smiling, barely able to form her words but working very hard to make herself understood. "I couldn't expect anything better than this."

As my heart rejoiced, my eyes teared and my body tension released. Could this be acceptable for her in the short term? She was willing to give every effort from her small five-foot body to this last chance, to live and be a little mobile.

I saw a strong, but frail woman, who had faced death and wanted to overcome and live. She was willing to take on a change of environment she'd previously detested, and to be flexible and adapting, just as people who overcome obstacles in accidents and life challenges do in order to endure.

And so I went home to Idaho once again. After a day, my exhausted muscles stopped shaking. It rained, and I enjoyed my paradise, tackling things quickly and knowing I would probably be called to California again shortly. I looked out my loft window at billowy clouds and intermittent rain, the spring snow threatening. Just another typical day in Idaho.

A cloth I used to clean my windows from the winter storm outside lay limp on the grass where I left it after the last urgent call from Hal. "You must come now. I need you, and your mother needs you." He was frantic in his wish to make her better with the appearance of her loving daughter.

Hal called me to California once again; I desperately tried to connect with reality before I went to Mom's house. I walked the streets of Los Gatos, a nearby town, touching live things—foliage, dogs—and chatting with people. I wanted three minutes of life before I visited my tortured mom and my inability to assist, or to help in her recovery. I was just trying to survive my mom's ordeal, trying to find light.

I passed an aged invalid woman, slumped in a wheelchair, being taken for a morning stroll. A second woman, probably about the same age, passed me at a slow jog, full of life's abundance. What happened to each to make this contrast? Can we change life's course through optimistic thoughts, exercise, or spiritual connection, or are we each on our own path from birth?

Once Mom returned home, she rediscovered moments of contentment, enjoying what she describes as "my wonderful English garden" that Hal made her. She views the world from her bed, framed by her den curtains, as her muscles erode. When I ask how she manages such a positive attitude, she tells me, "It is my world now, and I have lots of time to think and remember."

I wouldn't trade the special moments I've shared with her, and I feel honored to have this time with her presence. Maybe this is a typical passing, but it's a long and painful one for all involved.

With her German stubbornness, strength, zest, and family interactions, Mom is at peace with her simple life. Her story is an amazing gift to me. I've learned to never give up on a person. I question my prior support for euthanasia. We never know what is around the corner, and there's always a possibility for a miraculous recovery, as my smart brother and sister knew.

My journey with Mom is not what I expected. At one point, I thought of praying to God for her to die. She said that was what she wanted. But then, her inner will to live surfaced. She fought each medical emergency with a vengeance, reveling at the peak until the next trough appeared.

I was wrong to want death to relieve her pain. She surprised me, persevered, and found a level of enjoyment from her bed. Getting off her medication has allowed her to fight.

Survivors don't talk about how difficult situations are, but about how beautiful. This is what I hear from her now. Survivors take their thoughts to another world for refuge, and she has found that place of acceptance. She has surrendered to her situation because she has no other choice. By readjusting her perception of what is important and pleasurable in her current life, she is happy.

Mom continues to talk about getting out of bed to walk someday, and she lifts her arms and legs for a minute of exercise each day. Right now, that's all she can reach for. Yet her will to live is extraordinary.

She is alive after fourteen years of hospital crises and serene in the comforts of her bedridden world. She and Hal had wished for just a few magical years when they married at the advanced age of eighty. They have reaped much more than that. They are a loving couple, just keepin' on.

I asked myself why Mom has survived so many medical situations that could have ended her life, and why she chooses life over death as she fights to remain in this world. I came to the conclusion that she felt wanted, even needed, as she supports her children and husband in many ways from her "office" bed. She listens, she advises when asked, she loves, and she feels her family's love in return.

As I grow older, I think of how many more refrigerators, washers, and cars I should financially plan to buy in my lifetime. There is an urgency to make it all work. I asked Mom about this, but she replied with a surprising answer. "Oh, I never think of the future. I am concerned with my living now."

Maybe that is our answer—living in the now, without even knowing what phase of life we are in.

6

Down on Their Luck

～

*Sometimes, we don't know where our life path will lead.
Writing Mom's story showed me that there was an inner
strength buried in the body and soul of an older woman, aided
by her family, who just wasn't ready to throw in the towel.*

*But not everyone wins in life. I'm including the next two
chapters about people who greatly touched me as I
examined those who lose. I will try to discern why they
struggled so. What could we do to help them recover?
What part does a zest for and celebration of life play,
beyond basic survival? Both these women suffered from
not what they expected. Maybe that is what survival
is about — recovering from the unexpected.*

～

To ESCAPE THE HECTIC PACE OF MY HIGH-tech job, I frequently took what I called "mental health days," calling in sick to get precious time away from the stress, thus preserving my sanity a bit longer.

In 1999, on one of those days, I had an experience that changed my perception of hard times and our responsibilities to our fellow humans, including those we barely know. I also saw how an entire family, down on their luck, can display courage.

Frustrated by seventy-hour workweeks, I needed to escape for a long weekend. Driving my Z3 convertible from San Francisco to Santa Rosa was pleasant, despite the aggravation of stop-and-go traffic, and I felt sun kissed as I sat with the top down. I had eagerly packed some gourmet food, my tent, blankets, and just a fraction of the work that I would normally accomplish on my weekend.

As evening approached, I learned that the camp-ground where I'd planned to stay was closed because of a major storm. The only other one in the area was a filthy few acres where it appeared no maintenance had been done for years. I was greeted by a toothless person who explained his situation: "I escaped from Silicon Valley four years ago, and I'm now living in a laminated abode with six cats and a scummy partner." I wondered if this was what my job might also push me to someday.

There was no running water because of the recent flooding. I looked around, trying to be positive while muck caked my boots. Fees paid, I was now committed.

I drove through the campground, looking for a spot. I noticed many groups of unkempt and poorly dressed gray-haired men. Each man smiled as I drove by in my fire-engine-red car, but I kept going until I spotted a family. They had two tents, presumably for the parents and one for the children. I thought this location would be safer.

Outside their tents was a makeshift kitchen with wood stacked by a Weber barbeque and some cheap nylon lounge chairs. I introduced myself to the father, who must have noticed me looking at his woodpile. The cold wind whipped and pushed my hair into my face as he said, "Our winter wood supply hasn't arrived yet, so I bring this home from the construction site where I work." I started to realize that this might not be a weekend outing for the family.

He followed up with, "I'll sell you some for this chilly evening if you want."

As I set up camp, I heard the commotion of parents putting their dingy-faced young children to bed. Knowing little ones can push you to extremes, I assumed that Mom and Dad, tired from a day of camping, were exhausted. Yet I was surprised to realize that the noise was a melodic rendition of *Old MacDonald Had a Farm*, with Daddy leading and the children joyfully chiming in.

Despite the howling wind and my tent's rebellion, I got set up before dark. After cooking dinner, I retreated to my shelter and tried to get warm. I could barely move my frigid fingers to write as the wind whipped the nylon sides of my new tent. Although it was mid-May in California, the unusually nasty cold gripped me.

I got little rest that night, and realized that two polyester blankets on top of my old sleeping bag just weren't sufficient for this climate. Next time I would bring a wool cover, or maybe it was time to purchase a new bag that was adequate for California's spring.

As the sun rose, I decided to move on to somewhere warmer and safer. I lay in my tent, trying to find an excuse to get up and face the blistering cold. As I rested, I listened to the conversation next door. The children were crying, not wanting Daddy to leave for work. Mom screamed. Dad screamed. He needed to leave *right now* or he'd be late for his job.

Finally, he drove off in the old, beat-up vehicle I'd noticed parked at the site.

I dragged myself out of my tent and saw a two-year-old with golden locks. She walked around the campsite sucking a filthy bottle, her dirty diaper slipping down. Her four-year-old brother teased her and ran circles around her through the tall grass. In the frosty morning chill, their cries of frustration and hunger mixed with Mom's aggravation. She yelled "stop" and "behave" to no effect.

The two ruffians ran off toward a creek, and Mom slowed down to relax and contemplate a day anew.

Although I didn't usually do anything like this, I decided to engage. What I heard from her lips shocked me.

The family had lost their landscaping business to a corrupt partner, and as a result they were homeless. She emphasized *homeless* as she stared at my BMW. She said, "You know anyone, even you, could be homeless, anytime." Even while I acknowledged her statement, I didn't truly understand. She persisted. "Most people don't believe how easy it can happen."

I stared at her weathered face as she told me she was thirty-nine- years old. Her husband had just hawked her two-carat diamond ring so they could buy diapers and food for the baby. But she asserted, "I'll get it back soon." She was sure. Her parents lived on an exclusive Healds-burg ranch nearby, but she had declared her indepen-dence and refused to move in with them. She spoke as her red hands sloshed diapers around in a kettle of boiling water in the chilly air.

I asked if she thought about leaving the children in day care and working. "No," she said. She had two injured spinal discs and could only be on her feet for a short period at a time before needing to recline. She was trying to get disability insurance. Doctors had told her she could never work again, but it was difficult to get authorization for the assistance.

She adamantly declared, "We will make it," even as the chilly breeze ruffled her hair and the wrinkles edged a bit deeper into her tanned, leathery skin.

She watched every move as I packed my gear in the sports car to leave, and stared at the contents in my trunk.

I followed her gaze, desperately trying to think of something I could give this woman to help.

I thought back on our conversation. She was proud and would not accept help from her own parents, so I decided against offering the small amount of cash I had. It would be an insult, and probably wouldn't really affect her lifestyle. Instead, I thought about a book my friend Marilyn had just given me, called *Tough Times Never Last, But Tough People Do*. I had started reading it the previous night, and it was very inspiring.

This would be my gift. This woman seemed to be the reason I had received the book and why I was staying in this crummy campground. I asked if she had time to read for herself with her parental duties. Her eyes lit up when she saw the title. She told me, "I love books and reading, and this gift means so much to me."

How had a family spiraled to this depth? Was it just the economic times, or was it their inability to adjust to financial changes quickly enough? They were just responding, not actively managing them.

Most people would not suspect they lived at a campground if they saw this family in town, all cleaned up. Their plight was not outwardly apparent. These are the families in the U.S. who go to bed hungry, and who forego medical care. Too often, due to their transient life, these are the children who drop out of school.

I was concerned about the children, exposed to poverty for a long period of time. I had no way of ascertaining how long this family had been or would be in this situation. But I knew their children's health could be severely affected (heart disease, high blood pressure, metabolic syndrome). Studies show that the longer time a person is in poverty, the more severe their symptoms become, not to mention the psychological repercussions.

How long would this family remain in limbo? I saw their courage, but they had no zest for life — they were living at the bare minimum, which doesn't offer the fullness of survival.

Sometimes we need to accept or seek out help from others, which this family was not doing. They did not seem able to change their course. A more active pursuit of social services may have helped.

7

A Lost Soul

∽

When I met Kiki, she was headed in the direction of death. It is so hard for me to write that, as I care for her deeply even though I knew her intimately for just a few days. She still seems to be in my mind daily. I worry about her with such sadness. She is one more example of how a person can challenge survival, hanging on by a thread until it breaks.

∽

Upon arriving in Athens, Greece, during a backpacking trip, I set out to find the inexpensive hostel where I would stay for a few days before moving on to the sun-kissed Greek islands.

I arrived, exhausted, near my hostel at dusk, disembarking from the train I'd taken directly from the airport. I knew immediately no one would want to linger in this area. This was not a secure place to stay. I needed to be inside a safe place soon. The drug-addled men in the filthy, trash-laden streets surrounding my hostel could be bad for me unless I was ever vigilant and not out after dark. I found the welcome sign of International Hostel flapping over the front door, stepped into the lobby, and felt safe again.

After registering in the grimy hostel and climbing a flight of stairs, I unlocked the door to my dorm and found my roommate, Kiki. Dressed in a black negligee, she was laughing and acting bizarre. All of her worldly goods were strewn around her. This was her home in poverty, for now. She seemed very confused when I entered, and we talked briefly about her heartfelt sadness. A controlling former husband in Paris had forced her to sign business licenses and loans on two hotels he bought from money he extracted from her mother's property.

He'd convinced Kiki to use the equity to finance new properties, then expelled her from their apartment two years ago. He'd reneged on the loans in her name. He refused to give her any of the money or profits from the hotels. Her eleven-year-old daughter was living with him, and he'd poisoned her against Kiki. He would not allow visitation. The girl now refused any connection with her mom, not even phone calls.

She was in a harried state.

Kiki had returned to Athens after a recent trip to Paris, where she had to plead with him for money. He refused, and now she looked for work, any kind of income to survive. She told me the only way she could raise money would be to sell her recently deceased mother's home and restaurant on a Greek island. She had just engaged a lawyer, who would work on a retainer to pursue the case.

I told her the only possible solution I saw was for her to sell the inherited property immediately and hope for some gain, but the mortgage arrears were rapidly increasing and foreclosure would soon be a fact. Then she could sue her ex-husband. Yet Kiki seemed unable to move in any direction. Inability to act, I later recognized, is a major reason people lose. I later learned that the man was not legally her husband; they'd had a common-law marriage that turned abusive. He attacked her physically for twelve years before kicking her out with no money. She was drowning.

I left for dinner, embarrassed to lock up my stuff after we'd established this on-the-fly relationship of personal sharing just one short hour after meeting. I decided to take my cash, passport, and credit cards and leave the rest unlocked, up for grabs if she needed my things that badly. After I left, though, I regretted not securing my remaining items. Kiki was desperate at this point.

As I opened our room door to leave, Kiki warned how dangerous the area was, and how alert I must be. That was no news to me, a seasoned traveler.

Kiki got a call from a prospective restaurant employer who wanted to interview her. Her spirits lifted for the moment, and she dressed in tight black jeans, an equally tight-fitting black tank top with lace, and a black belt with silver thorns. It was not the interview outfit I would wear.

She rushed out, but returned shortly, back in her depressed mode, dressed once again in a lacy black nightgown. Her scraggily black hair fell to her shoulders as she curled her scrawny body on her bunk. The man she met wanted her to work in another town. She would not do this, because she had tried a similar arrangement in the past when she was desperate for work. She'd spent the little money she had left to get there and then … she did not tell me the rest. I gave her a pep talk and sent her out to ask different establishments for work, suggesting a target of a least three contacts a day. I threw in a lecture about how she needed to sell her house before the bank took control of the assets. We hang on too long when strife hits, going through our savings, and we do not think clearly. She needed to act now, without wishes or dreams.

Kiki had no degree, had worked only menial jobs, and had no money to support herself. She was not even paying for the dorm room, but was under the impression that her lawyer, who brought her there, was. In her mind, she was safe for the moment. She didn't know when the hostel might ask her to leave or what she would be required to do to repay her lawyer's favor. She needed to face reality. Maybe she had, and this is what it was.

Tough lessons.

The next day, after sightseeing and a delicious gyro with tzatziki sauce from a street vendor, I returned to my room. Kiki was there, looking dejected, so I suggested we go down to the breakfast room and talk.

Kiki desperately waited for a phone call that would save her, and always kept the cell next to her in the bunk or in her hand. A male friend in Paris who said he would come to Athens to help might contact her; he never called. "But who knows," she said, as she continued to wait with hope.

She also waited for a call about a job. A man she met on the street offered her a position caring for his elderly mother. She had initially turned him down, but now was reconsidering. He wanted to meet her at the metro at 9:00 that evening and take her somewhere to talk. She mulled it over and decided it was too dangerous. I asked, "Why at night, in the dark?" She agreed. If he called, she would tell him she could meet him in the daylight. It did not sound like a real job offer to me, but she was in dire need.

There were also a couple of hotels that "might interview me," she mentioned enthusiastically. But when she'd returned to them with my encouragement, both requested she come back when the manager was in, which was a polite Greek way to say no. She searched the newspapers, spending her last change to purchase them, with no positive results.

Kiki had nightmares of her ex cutting off her legs. He had called while I was out and made that specific threat: if she ever returned to Paris and tried to see her daughter, he would "break both her legs and cut them off." Kiki cried, tears rolling down her pale cheeks. She had no doubt he would hire someone to do this. Looking in her eyes, I believed her.

As we talked, I naively encourage her to find a free class to learn computer skills. She told me she had not been able to find any instruction that did not charge. I ask about social programs to help displaced housewives. She did not know of any in Athens, only in other countries.

Greece was poor, a dramatic contrast to the empire of past centuries that ruled a huge portion of the world.

Watching Kiki's panic and inability to focus was extremely gloomy, and I, too, began losing hope for her recovery.

Traumatic events like the ones Kiki had encountered leave a person emotionally challenged for years. She felt helpless, threatened, as safety and stability were ripped away. I saw Kiki's phases of fear and anxiety, which caused pain and grief.

How each person reacts to these events depends on their perception of what is happening, and on their previous experience of trauma, their coping abilities, and their levels of existing support. With multiple traumas, it takes longer to recover. I saw Kiki on this downward path as it became more difficult for her to deal with each occurrence.

We can't always control the events in our lives, but we can control how we perceive them and respond. Grieving restores balance in life, and it is very important to reach out to others for support, but Kiki wouldn't.

Her parents were dead, she had no siblings, and apparently, for whatever reason, no friends. I believed she was an anorexic, depressed person, along with her other problems.

It was difficult to not be able to help further, when I feared the result of doing nothing. Yet I gave her my spiritual tools, and looking back I guess that was all I could do. I encouraged her to use the Internet to get to my website—a contact point that would require her to learn some computer skills. She told me the fellow at the hostel desk would show her. She'd need to be motivated enough and have the ability to think clearly.

I bought an omelet one morning for breakfast at the hostel, then lied and told Kiki I could not finish it. Could she help by eating half? "Oh no," she insisted several times. I knew she was only eating the free bread, jam, and coffee offered at the hostel each day, but she was just too proud. So there went my omelet in the trash while my stomach growled.

Kiki and I talked about our personal sadness and triumphs. I felt bonded with her survival. Kiki encouraged my dreams, and said I would write the travel articles and eventually my book. I hold on to that faith. I reiterated that she would find a job and survive. It was a difficult challenge to know, to see, but not to find the key for helping. My moroseness grew.

Upon leaving, I left a twenty dollar bill on her dresser. This woman was spiraling downward. Each day was worse than the previous, and my twenty dollars might have been all that was left in her world. She had become dependent on others' gracious help, with very little hope for a future.

Kiki was worn down, worn out. Emotions can drain you of life essence, depleting the possibility of recovery at a tipping point. What was her next move—prostitution? Death? I never heard from her again. I tried to contact the hostel to learn of her, but was not able to find an answer.

Change is difficult, but often essential to survival. Kiki seemed incapable of it. She was a lost soul, a person who will most likely challenge survival, at best.

A note about one of Kiki's challenges:

In 2010, when I travelled to Athens, the unemployment rate in Greece was astronomical (more than 50 percent), with work almost impossible to find. Single women were especially hard hit, with the added insult of a deteriorating health-care system. Greeks rebelled against financial reforms with frightening strikes and protests that I witnessed daily when traveling there. Despondency permeated the society. It was a mess. Up to four hundred thousand people a day relied on street soup kitchens. By 2012, suicide rates had increased 40 percent over previous years, and twenty thousand were homeless. Today, the story is worse.

8

The Miracle

～

As I wrote about struggling with little hope, I wanted to find the positive alternative.

This next story and "The Fighter" chapter have much in common — a will to live, persistence, and confinement. With the ability to overcome and connect to what lies ahead, Ed's realm becomes more precious.

～

ED WAS DECLARED DEAD ON DECEMBER 13, 2013 by the attending doctor, following a six-hour open-heart surgery two weeks before.

"No!" screamed his daughter.

"Yes," the doctor reiterated. "It is time to remove the tubes that are artificially allowing him to breathe." His daughter insisted he was not dead, and said no, the tubes could not—would not—be removed.

This sixty-five-year-old Vietnam vet had endured much in his life. In addition to his wartime experiences, Ed battled the cancerous effects from his service to his country, overcoming by visualizing those nasty white cells being conquered by the reds. He rose above and won. Chemo and radiation therapies were partners in his life. He found the way to keep going. He ardently worked out, lifting weights with a positive outlook.

This allowed him to go on to the next battle, but the emotions in his life ceased as if sucked from his being. He built a wall between himself and everyone he loved when he was struck with illness, and post-traumatic stress disorder (PTSD) ravished his mind with horrible night-mares in the dark. He withdrew into his protective shell against the world, against any feelings, against real life. In his mind, it was the only way he could continue to live, but it wasn't really living.

Did he have any idea what he became, devoid of emotions and unable to have deep connections? He moved through each day confidently communicating with others, but on a relationship level, he always stopped.

Stopped before he imploded.

He gave unconditional love to the only beings he could, his dogs. Animals would not injure him; they were safe.

He walked through life not knowing what carnage was ravaging inside him.

Working out one day, he noticed how quickly he was out of breath. This continued for some time. Was it a result of aging? Was it another cancer alert? Eventually, close to collapse, he checked with a doctor. They discovered his heart was not functioning as it should. He was constantly deprived of oxygen.

After test upon test, the diagnosis was made. He had blockages that required heart surgery. This was something he could not exercise or visualize into oblivion. It was a medical condition necessitating surgical intervention.

Surgery is pretty frightening stuff for anyone, but Ed had no idea just how seriously this situation would develop. He didn't know he would be fighting for his life and his ability to think.

On November 25, Ed's life changed. The initial operation was successful, but longer than expected. Now it was up to him to struggle back, to help his body repair. Vietnam was nothing compared to this; failed relationships were inconsequential; cancer battles were no longer relevant. Ed just never woke from his operation, never saw the barrage of family standing by to wish him a speedy recovery.

The next day, Ed continued to sleep. A doctor or nurse mentioned the word "coma" to the ever-attentive family. He was far away from our known world with little awareness of what was occurring each day and night. To him, the passage of time was nonexistent. Where the heck was he? No one knew; he just was not here in the now.

Days passed. Weeks passed.

His aspiration rate fell from 90 to 70. It needed to be 30 before they could remove the breathing tube, which could only remain in his body for ten days. If things didn't improve, they would need to do a tracheotomy. He was on twenty-four-hour watch with the hospital staff.

His brother, Collin, insisted that Ed's daughter come to Southern California from Oregon. He told her things looked serious. Only Ed's direct family was allowed to visit in order to protect his dignity while a tangle of tubes drained from various body parts.

Ed was a cherished friend, and I was also fighting for his existence from a distance of two states away. With all the strength I could conjure, I allowed my spiritual angels to protect him as I visualized him winning this new battle for his life.

Doctors kept him sedated to control his erratic movements and give his heart time to heal. At one point he thrashed, likely from violent nightmares, and pulled out all his tubes. Eventually the hospital resorted to white cotton gloves on his hands, tied to the bed's metal rail, incapacitating him from repeating an act that could cause death.

Ed's sisters arrived, and the family started to talk about how he'd wish to die. Should they pull the plugs? Do heroic measures to sustain a vegetable? Then after, what did he want—cremation, burial in a plot, a funeral? Maybe cremation was best, with his ashes scattered on the ocean he loved and surfed for years. How should they distribute his life possessions? Why had their loved one, lying now in a hospital bed and wrapped in a steel-blue blanket, left no directives, no living will? Life was now a confining straitjacket in so many ways.

Slowly, their acceptance of the inevitable came.

When I called Collin, he reported the facts without emotion. He was drained from exhibiting so much in the last weeks. I heard the resignation, his voice as sterile as if reporting a news story of someone else's relative. "Ed's condition has not changed." I cringed. Was it the same as "still dying" or the same as "Ed's oxygen level not increasing?" It sounded ominous.

Three weeks after his surgery, Ed was declared dead.

But no, his daughter and I were two, fighting for his life, not resigned to letting him slip away. We knew this man intimately. He wouldn't give up, nor would we. No plugs would be pulled, his daughter commanded. She climbed onto his bed and held her daddy like he was her baby. Maybe, just maybe, Ed felt her presence, her extreme caring. Their closeness.

Ed had someone from his family with him daily, as well as his daughter's emotional support, which seemed to help him pull through the ordeal. Words of encouragement help patients rally, even though we think they are not aware in their unconscious state.

Some people in comas see aberrations or lights; they feel they have died and are ascending to heaven. Are they arriving back here when they wake, returning from a state of suspension until their destination is reestablished here on earth?

I read an article from Washington University's School of Medicine, which said that 2.4 percent of men have neurological events following surgery — a stroke, TIA, or coma. Strange things happen when people are in a coma, and we all react differently. Some are not conscious of visitors' conversations or words, while others remember portions after waking. But all have a positive effect. For Ed, it was like he was in a black hole.

A week before Christmas they performed Ed's tracheotomy, and they lowered his high dose of sedatives to a point where he slowly started to wake. He was paralyzed. He couldn't swallow, and he took shallow breaths. An infection ravished his body, and his vocal cords were not working.

Collin maintained a daily vigil when he could get to the hospital from his home miles north. He sometimes sat outside Ed's room, and one day he noticed a woman he did not know walk in. He told Ed later that she never came out, although the room had only one door.

Christmas season was celebrated even in this place of life and death. Carolers roamed the halls, singing uplifting music. Later, when Ed was released and we met, he told me something strange. He remembered a woman entering his room. When he opened his eyes, she stood by his bed, singing carols to him. He knew she was an angel. It made him feel peaceful. As he relayed the story, tears welled in his eyes. This was not a religious or emotional man. What was happening to him?

Ed's oxygen moved from 90 to 60. That was better, but it needed to register 30 percent before they could take his trach tube out. Ed remained somewhat sedated and in a semicoma state.

On Christmas Eve, I got an amazing present. Collin called: "Ed can't talk yet on the phone, but he is making eye contact and he's awake! He's in intensive care." Ed could breathe on his own, despite the tracheotomy.

Two weeks later, he was making progress but quarantined with pneumonia, which was followed by staph and MRSA infections. His family reported that he was confused; he could remember the past but couldn't make present memories, and he couldn't eat or drink. The good news was that he was speaking normally. The tubes were only in his nose. He could sit in a chair and breathe on his own.

Progress.

I began to worry about what his mental state would be after the multiple medical interventions. His family reported recent visits from a psychologist. Why were they evaluating him? Could he move forward to recovery, to the person he was?

But still, miracles happen. He is alive. Thank you, angels!

After months of negative reports, a conversation with Collin was hopeful. "They moved him to the Menlo Park VA facility for rehab. His pneumonia and other infectious diseases have mostly cleared, as well as his mind."

Collin still had to remind him each visit, "No, what you are talking about was a dream. Come back to reality, to what is happening now." It seemed to be working. The support that Ed received from his brother and Collin's wife, Vickie, was amazing.

Finally, Ed called me. He sounded alert, and his familiar voice shocked me. No one would guess the two-month ordeal he had just experienced. He talked about the violent, horrible, disturbing dreams he'd had while in a coma. He'd seen himself drowning, suffocating in the dark depths of a river. His arms and back ached, and he was sure someone had beaten him.

He also told me about a *wonderful* meal of chicken pot pie he'd gotten on his second day in the VA facility, but then they moved him to another place that served only mush. He was refusing to eat it, and wondered if McDonald's delivers.

Ed called again after he was up and walking. For some reason, he couldn't move forward, so he'd taken one thousand steps (two times around his facility) walking backwards. I thought it was kind of funny, but tried not to giggle while we were talking. I didn't know if this brain deficiency was temporary or not.

Ed still couldn't use his arms at all. He was exhausted, and he'd lost forty pounds, most of which was muscle mass. He told me that his muscles had decreased from 80 percent to an alarming 20 percent, mostly owing to the long weeks in a coma-state fetal position. He wasn't strong enough to use a wheelchair. He had a long fight ahead of him.

Speaking with him was amazing. I never thought Ed would be able to talk to me again. His voice, always low and velvety, sounded just the same as I remembered, and it pleased me to chat with this brave and special man. I didn't care if he walked backward. I was celebrating his movement, his spirit to conquer this thing he had undergone, his essence.

Ed just kept moving through life with a positive attitude. Willing himself to live and ignoring pain, continuing with his ever-present exercise programs and meditation, he overcame, just as he had always done.

Ed's emotional box, the walls that had protected him from feelings for the twenty-five years we'd been friends, were now broken. He cried when I told him how lucky he was to have such a devoted brother who stood by him, no matter what. Collin had protected Ed against any perceived annoyance, interference to his progress, or damage to his fragile mental state during his struggle.

Ed realized, in a way he never had before, how important his brother was to him. He finally allowed all the feelings of his life to actualize in his brain, his body, and his soul. It was amazing to see the new growth. All that he suffered and overcame was worth that one moment.

He had returned to the real world—or perhaps he was here, fully, for the first time in years.

In the following weeks he started to text me from his phone in a coherent manner. I was delighted. He sounded bored with hospital food and accommodations, and ready to move on. He was using his wheelchair and walking, surprising the staff with his rapid progress.

One day, he reported that he almost had a catastrophe while sitting in his wheelchair. He gathered speed rolling down a ramp toward a wall that required a sharp and immediate left turn to avoid. Ed did a wheelie to make it, but he soon realized he must control his exuberance and slow down. He graduated to walking forward, holding onto the guardrails for one hundred feet at a time.

He described a beautiful lady with long, silky legs and high red heels walking past his room. He felt something. He was coming back.

What was he fighting for? Why was his survival possible and forward progress so rapid? That spirit I heard when we talked confirmed my thoughts. "As soon as I am released," he said, "I will go to the local gym, and I'll walk around my neighborhood daily to get back to normal."

Why has he lived through this ordeal, I asked? "Because I have a desire to live life and never give up."

Ed still did not remember any of his visitors during his coma except the angel, but with time, snippets of conversations with visitors may surface.

Four months after entering the hospital, he was walking three miles on a treadmill and pushing himself to go farther. He had gained eighteen pounds since surgery. His doctor calls him a miracle.

Ed still has obstacles to conquer. His mind still focuses on the past, but slowly, he allows some present experiences to emerge. I am sure that he will continue to overcome with time.

His brother and sisters smartly closed up his apartment while he was hospitalized, and moved his possessions to storage. Now, upon release from the hospital, Ed can start a new life; he's free to go in any direction. That can be an overwhelming decision, choosing which path to explore.

As those people who are close to me pass on, I visually put them in a whitewater raft with Michael, who you met in Chapter 1 and who died two years ago. It makes me smile to see him up there somewhere having the time of his life with the people I loved most. I'm thankful not to offer Ed to the raft just yet, though. I'm glad he's still on earth, where I can have the pleasure of seeing and touching him.

Ed has always been a warrior, with a strong passion for life, and he persisted in his goals. He had a lot of people willing him to live and prayers sent his way and my angels. Does this help one to survive?

9

A Preemie's Struggle

～

*These intimate stories of mine share many of the same
components. Ed's family's support became an important
reason he pulled through, back to the living. The same is
true for the babies in the next story. I had never guessed
the strong connections that my fellow humans have
that enable a continuation of life. Often, survival is the
result of support from those who love them deeply.*

～

IN THE TOWN OF ESCONDIDO, CALIFORNIA, surrounded by the smell of ocean breezes, I sat in a coffee house made mostly of large, open windows, with almost no walls in sight. It reminded me of lodge homes I'd enjoyed in the Amazon.

I moved across the worn mahogany floor, grooved from years of wear and spilled brew, inhaling the smell of coffee from my cup. It was early morning, and the soft, angular sunrays fought to enter the room along with the birds daily looking for a handout. The shop was packed with caffeine junkies who just wanted their morning jolt to help move them into action for the day.

Soon I was in conversation with a woman I'd never met before. She told me a story similar to one I experienced myself some years ago. I often think about this personal survival story, and the tears flow no many how many times I relive it or try to understand what happened.

Christine's son was born in the sixth month of her pregnancy. This was twenty years ago, when premature babies born in the second trimester often did not live long. They succumbed to oxygen deprivation or other major issues, and those who did live often had lifelong medical challenges.

Doctors prepared Christine's family for the inevitable—their son would soon be dead. Girls had a higher percentage of preemie survival, for some reason. But this was a male.

Christine's response that day and every day for the six months that followed—was that he *would* live, and he *would* be healthy. The baby fought as the doctors worked to keep his lungs from collapsing. He had a stroke. Yet on and on he fought for his life, as did his family.

The baby boy was welcomed by four older brothers—ages eleven, nine, eight, and seven. He was a very small bundle, weighing in at just one and a half pounds, and he could fit in Christine's curved hand with space left. From the day his four brothers met him in the Neonatal Intensive Care Unit (NICU), this baby was loved, encouraged to push forward, and allowed to make his own place in their family and world. He struggled in the hospital, and he fought. Every day his brothers read to him, brought tapes to play for him, and showed him their art to stimulate a reaction.

He was left with cerebral palsy from the stroke he had when first born; it impaired his movement and normal development. When he learned to roll over on his back, his arms and legs flailed; it was almost impossible for him to reverse that action and get back on his stomach, but his brothers were always there to assist.

The doctors said he would never walk. His mother wouldn't accept that diagnosis, either. The brothers, knowing him to be just one of them, taught him how to run, and how to overcome the physical disabilities. They taught him to conquer his shortcomings.

That boy now walks through life, not as one but as five. No one gave up on this child—ever.

As he grew, his athletic brothers taught him sports, and they taught him about life. Christine's baby is now a grown man with a job. He suffers pain daily, but he never complains. He is a functioning adult and gives to others spiritually. He is a contributor to this world and an amazing story of survival.

My granddaughter was also born prematurely due to HELLP Syndrome. She entered our world five weeks before her due date. At four and a half pounds, she seemed impossibly small the first time I saw her in the hospital. Wires and tubes emanated from all parts of her body. Her lungs had collapsed, and everyone around her felt she would die.

I arrived, after driving across states like a maniac, intending to say my good-byes, to ask the powers to gently take this miniature angel someplace wonderful, where she could grow and play in the heavens. At that time in my life I knew little about spirituality, but I tried to grasp something that was beyond me, that might help her live.

I arrived in a room full of what appeared to be rows of clear plastic storage carriers. Each contained a baby who just wasn't supposed to enter the world when they did. A name was prominently printed above each baby's head with a black marker, and the mundane detail seemed to signify something more—the children's defiant existence, even for what might be a very short time on our planet, as a unique newborn.

I walked to my own granddaughter and could not believe what a flawless, beautiful, naked baby girl I saw.

Yes, she was tiny and thin, but such perfectly formed fingers and toes—her nails the size of a large dot on each hand and foot. I knew at that moment that I would help her to fight to live.

I focused, sending powerful waves of energy, hope, and angels to help her with her fight. I didn't know what those might be. I had no familiarity with all this stuff at the time. Yet it was too important to not find a way, from every cell in my body and mind, for this baby to live. I would try anything.

I was allowed to stay in the room by her, in her beautiful presence, for only a few minutes, but I knew that I was doing something to help her survival. Although I wasn't a religious person, I began my journey to find the power of spirituality and healing.

I told Christine my story. We both cried, not noticing or caring that others around us may not understand two women who had such love, hope, and determination for their children's futures. We were exchanging one of our best life experiences.

I often think about why my granddaughter survived. I now think of Christine's son. One reason might be the determination and love of supporters surrounding these fragile souls. I believe we can affect the universe and path of our loved ones through positive thoughts and something people often don't understand—our spiritual interactions.

10

Can I Survive the Jungle?

~

Babies and families fight for their right, their place, in our society, but how does spiritual connection assist with survival?

This next story talks about the magic that can be revealed and appreciated when we're not distracted by everyday occurrences, and we surrender. Maybe letting go and experiencing extremes in a crisis is a gift. Sometimes you can't do anything but accept the present and see where your path leads. Can a life-threatening experience actually become a gift that feeds us going forward? I'd never thought about survival circumstances in those parameters, with those benefits.

~

ANNETTE HERFKENS RELISHED TIME AWAY from her stressful job. She loved her work, but the demands were rigorous, with little opportunity to take time off. She was looking forward to a renewing break, lounging on the beaches of Vietnam with her fiancé of thirteen years.

The thirty-one-year-old woman always strove to excel. Annette was raised in the Netherlands and studied law, then was employed in various banking positions as she climbed the corporate ladder. Her contemplative personality allowed her to assess the scope of a situation, consider options, and move ahead to solve business issues. But, she needed—no, she *and* her fiancé needed—a break from their hectic work schedules.

Standing on the Ho Chi Minh City tarmac, in Vietnam, she considered the small Russian Yakovlev Yak-40 jet that was supposed to take them to their resort. It was 1992—why were they still flying such an old plane? She hesitated. She hated flying. The small plane held only about twenty-five passengers, but her fiancé assured her it would be just a puddle jump of twenty minutes to their destination. She would be basking in the sun in an hour.

After takeoff, she started to unwind, convinced that the flight would soon be over. She wouldn't make a fuss.

Ten minutes passed, and she noticed they were still climbing. "Shouldn't we be approaching the airport?" she asked. Her fiancé laughed and told her it was actually a fifty-five minute flight. He'd thought it would be easier for her to visualize a shorter flying experience.

As they got closer to their destination, the plane shuddered. Annette assumed it was an air current. She was the only passenger not wearing a seatbelt. Another shudder, this time more intense, and she realized that it was serious. She and her fiancé clutched hands, and she heard fear in his voice. Then they were falling, faster and faster, to the earth, until they were one with it. Annette remembers a searing sound, as the fuselage broke away from the plane, and then a wing. Smoke and flames consumed them.

They had crashed into a mountaintop.

All hell broke loose. Annette heard the moaning and screams, but she doesn't remember much more except the one thing that would break her heart and forever change her life. Her fiancé, sitting beside her, was dead. She knew it immediately, looking into his eyes. She was trapped under a seat with a dead man on top of her. She faded in and out of consciousness.

Annette was barely coherent, but she understood that she needed to get out of the plane, which was on fire. Somehow her will to live forced her into action despite her life-threatening injuries. Her lung was collapsed, her jaw broken, her hip fractured, and a four-inch bone protruded out of her flesh. She had numerous lacerations and wounds all over her body.

What drove her forward? Was it the inner strength revealed during her banking career, or maybe it was the adrenaline that masked some of the pain? Annette crawled, inch by inch, across the jungle floor, until she finally dropped her body and fainted in agony.

Upon awakening, she realized the gravity of her plight. They were in a dense jungle. There were bodies all around, and her fiancé was dead. She had to face it eventually, she knew, but for now she put that thought somewhere else in her mind, to deal with later. She instinctively knew that her focus must be in the present, moving forward to survive, or she would be dead as well. She struggled to accept her situation.

She could now feel the full brunt of her body's wreckage and pain. She would not allow it to control her; she knew she must control it. Annette assessed her situation and formulated a plan.

It is unusual for a trauma victim to be able to move so quickly into planning after an accident. Normally, after shock, a person struggles to accept their fateful situation, and it takes time to come to grips with reality before eventually moving ahead. But within minutes, Annette's mind was already there.

Her ability to accelerate the process allowed her to continue living while many around, who had survived the initial impact, were dying. She described it as mind over matter; she would only look at life, not death.

During the ensuing days, whenever she started to grieve, she stopped her emotions. That would be done in another place, another time.

Outside the plane, a few others were still alive. Most were moaning and crying, but they were also struggling to live. A kind Vietnamese man opened his suitcase with great effort to retrieve pants for her. She had lost hers in the crash and was wearing only underpants. This small gesture never left her mind; his compassion in a desperate situation, thinking of another human, touched her. The pants helped with the insects that attacked her wounds. She begged him not to leave her.

Days passed. All of the moans were silent, their struggles ended. Annette was alone in the jungle, the only survivor. Could she live until they found her? Was anyone even searching for the downed plane? She started to give up hope when no rescue aircraft flew overhead. The smell from the rotting flesh was disgusting, and the insects were eating the man beside her.

She forced herself not to cry; crying would make her even thirstier, she reasoned. Again, she chose to control her emotions.

Realizing she was the only one responsible for her survival, Annette focused her mind to extinguish all of her heart's emotions, and she forced herself to acknowledge and act on instincts that now guided her. This woman used her intuition and consciousness to keep herself alive. Mindfulness (living in the moment, not the past or present) can transform our awareness in a compelling way.

There was no food, but the one thing she could control in her situation was collecting rain water to drink.

You can live longer without food than water. Without food, it is possible for those in good physical shape to survive up to eight weeks. Food is stored as energy in the form of fat, carbohydrates, and proteins. Under stress, the body uses its reserves in that order. Annette's metabolism probably adjusted downward, as well, requiring less while she was trapped in a jungle wilderness with little physical exertion.

When it's hot, though, the body becomes dehydrated faster. A person must have water after three to seven days. In severe heat, like what Annette may have faced in the jungle, a body can lose up to 1.5 liters per day though sweating. Dehydration leads to eventual heat stroke and shock.

Annette's decision to collect water was absolutely the right thing to do at that time. She was fairly immobile, but with effort she could inch her body back to where the plane's wing lay and drink from the rain-saturated Styrofoam exposed inside the metal. During a downpour, Annette opened her mouth to the sky and drank the falling liquid.

As she lay on the moist forest floor, leeches moved in and out of her wounds. She tried to rub them off, but when she couldn't do that, she looked away. She would not allow them to frighten her.

Instead of concentrating on the grossness, Annette considered the beauty of a droplet of rain that rested on a mint-green leaf above her. The crystal of light refracting in her eyes was amazing, and she played with the shapes and colors in her view. She felt its glory. It was easier to focus on the jungle's splendor than the dead and decaying.

She drew energy from the splendor of the jungle. If she controlled her mind, she could control her emotions. She was not frightened. The daily rain washed over her body, and the canopy of leaves moved with the wind above her, almost in a mystical dance. She found delight in the sun's rays emanating to her being as if calling her body to live, giving her respite from the terrible horror and a piece of heaven on earth.

She reminded herself not to look down at the maggots, but continued to study the glorious birth and rebirth of nature surrounding her. She was now in bed with love, at peace, unified with joy and the universe.

She devised a plan. If, after six days, no one came, she would crawl through the jungle to find help. Having a plan allowed her to relax and conserve her energy. It was the complete opposite of the impatient person she had been her whole life. In the jungle, Annette felt protected, and she completely surrendered. She saw the secrets of life, and realized she was the secret.

This, amazingly, was her rescue. She was at peace, surrendering to what she had never known or thought about in her previous life.

When Annette was found in this impenetrable environment, eight days after the crash, she was just drifting permanently into that other, beautiful world. She really did not want to acknowledge her rescuers; they would remove her from this place of brilliance. She wasn't ready to leave the mystical space between death and life. Maybe she saw what we see when transitioning to the other side. She didn't want to return to reality.

The rescue team carried her in a makeshift sling, draped over poles, to her originally planned destination — the beach resort just twelve miles from the crash site. Annette's humor surfaced, and she laughed at the thought of herself as a roasted pig on a stick. It helps with survival to celebrate the absurd.

Annette spent long months in the hospital and recovery. It was sixteen weeks before she took her first step, but she didn't stop moving after that.

Her analytical mind could not comprehend the joyous place she lived during those days in the jungle. Thirteen years later, she returned to the site of her crash in 2014 to see if her vision of the surreal that guided her was true. What had happened on that mountain? What was that serene feeling of beauty and pleasure that kept her spirits in the present and allowed her to survive? There, at the crash site, she confirmed her higher spiritual connection in this world and searched for the meaning of life. This was a journey of closure.

Upon her return to Vietnam, she learned a second plane had vigilantly searched for the downed aircraft. This search plane also crashed into a mountain, and all seven on board were killed. Annette met with the tearful widows as they shared their grief.

Her reclaimed life led to marriage, two children, a continuing career, and benevolent gratitude for all she is and will be. This is a story of physical and psychological survival, and the depth it gives you. It was Annette's choice to focus on beauty and living, not death. From it, she received gifts, including a son with autism. Despite the challenges of this new voyage, the acknowledgement of her spiritual guides on the mountaintop help her rejoice in daily living.

Her book, *Turbulence*, a message of love, gains, and losses was released in 2014.

11

Homeless Girl

On top of the world with a great career, Annette Herfkens was going to set the world on fire with her passion for life, but experienced instead an abrupt change of direction. In minutes, she lost the love of her life and almost lost her own. She found peace, a way to fight back from the jungle floor and maintain her sanity. She strove to exist. Her hope and persistence moved her forward to do what she needed — to reach the water drips that nourished her body until the rescue team arrived, and she became one with her environment.

Homelessness is a different kind of threat. You become off balance, out of control. And if you are mobile, you are responsible for your own rescue. Brianna was in denial for eighteen months of her thirty-month homeless experience, but she was responsible for her own survival from the start.

IN 2008, BRIANNA KARP LOST HER JOB. She continued making her rent payments by doing temp work, but her income couldn't cover her expenses. She dipped into her savings until it, too, vanished. She got rid of most of her possessions and tried living with her parents; that didn't work.

Feeling she had only one option left, she moved into the decrepit trailer left by a deceased relative. The state of California ruled it uninhabitable, with no electrical power or running water.

Brianna was now the proud occupant of a piece of rusting metal in a Walmart parking lot. Her life had changed dramatically. She was borderline homeless, similar to the family in the campground we saw earlier. It is shockingly easy to slip through the cracks of society and see all that you've worked so hard for evaporate.

I have my own memories of Walmart's policy to let pretty much anyone park short-term in their lots. A boyfriend and I lived a quasi-gypsy life for a bit. I had a place to live, but he didn't. He would camp in the woods of Idaho, just pulling off the road at the end of a day. Through him, I learned there is a whole community of people who live day to day with what money they can gather for necessities. Many of them actually enjoy it.

Most of my boyfriend's areas to camp were free and in beautiful wilderness settings, often abutting roaring rivers. The drawback was that there was no electricity. Campers brought camp stoves and water, and they retired early. Traveling with him wasn't bad, and it was always an adventure.

We scraped up enough for a trip across the country and fixed up the back of his pickup truck with a bed shelf and room underneath for our "toys"—a tent, camp gear, and recreational equipment. It worked, and we toured the U.S. in an unusual sixty-day trip. There was little money in the budget for lodging; we certainly couldn't afford motels, regardless of the weather.

We started out looking for rest stops; they had bathrooms with sinks. Then we hit the jackpot and discovered Walmart parking lots. They were all across America, and they only asked that we keep our area neat. The best part, for me, was that their location in shopping areas meant that we were surrounded by bathrooms and nice restaurants. We joined a community of wanderers and started to recognize people. It reminded me of RV parks, where you see people from previous stops, all of them briefly settling and then moving on.

But back to Brianna's story.

This metal dump became her home. She went into survival mode, slashing her expenses to the bare minimum.

She'd go to a local Starbucks and use their Wi-Fi to apply for jobs, then get depressed, wondering why she was not able to move ahead. She missed her piano most.

She had to give up her huge Neapolitan mastiff, too; there was no way he could live in her hot trailer.

Without power, Brianna couldn't cook, and she started eating unhealthy food. Sleeping on the beat-up couch or floor did not give her good rest. And she missed her books and movies—furniture could always be replaced, she reasoned, but possibly not each hand-picked novel.

During her Starbucks excursions she discovered there were lots of homeless people online. Some of them slept outside, on benches or sidewalks, or they lived in cars, trying to blend in. Public libraries and government programs furnished them with computers. The Internet kept them connected to the outside world.

She learned that many homeless battle addiction and mental illness. Some were incarcerated and had no place to go when they were released.

I was staying with a friend in Florida who was rebuilding structures after a severe hurricane. Nine months before, Hurricane Charley had decimated much of Fort Meyers, causing thirteen billion dollars in damage. It still looked like a war zone when I arrived. Roofs were blown off, trash piled in heaps, and trees were all stripped down. Homes were completely destroyed by wind, water, or both. The citizens were mostly still waiting for federal funding, but some projects, like the one my friend worked on, had been approved.

My friend was temporarily sharing a single room with other workers, but there was no housing available for me. To make it worse, I had brought my one-hundred-pound, long-haired dog into the summer heat, not realizing the housing shortage.

We settled in a campground. It was not ideal, as we had only a small tent that I'd brought. We soon purchased a cooler to keep our food, a camp stove, and some plastic dishes. We ended up living there for more than three months of sweltering heat and humidity.

While my friend worked during the day, my dog and I roamed the town to stay occupied and cool, driving in the car and lingering in cheap restaurants. We were on a strict budget.

I saw a FedEx man establishing his turf under a palm tree and a small awning. This was temporary quarters—their building was a heap of rubble around the corner. Trucks gathered early in the morning to load boxes for the daily deliveries. Businesses go on, if you can find them.

Everywhere I went, people gathered to talk about the hurricane that devastated their city, even months later. They tried to handle the emotions of the event and purge their despair and sadness. They tried to move ahead, but for the moment they were stuck. It would be a long healing process.

In the tent at night, with the lights of the park barely illuminating "paradise," we settled after an exhausting day of heat. I could see the clothes I wore that day, limp with moisture. Washing the grease-stained, wrinkled T-shirt and jeans made no change to their grungy appearance. It seemed impossible to look like a normal person when I lived in a tent for long periods of time. There was all the dirt and grime blowing around, and the cramped storage of jumbled clothes spilling from a suitcase next to my floor mat and sleeping bag.

The lettuce I'd just purchased was brown when I pulled it out of the cooler for what would be our basic evening meal—a wilted salad.

Trying to remain positive, I found a portion of my soul slipping. I cleaned less; I cooked less; I was less concerned about my appearance. As I glanced in the mirror, I saw an older person wearing little makeup, her hair flipping every which way. Everything was less.

My friend and I bickered, having shared too many minutes together in a stressful situation. The day before, when we went out to breakfast at a restaurant, we hadn't talked at all.

Circumstances can erode your quality of life when you start a downward slide. Then depression seeps in, despite your efforts to repel it. Stress creates more stress and makes life so much harder to manage successfully. And the homeless don't even have the luxuries we had in this camp zone.

I met a truly homeless man, Bill, while I was in Florida. The experience gave me insight to the mentality of homelessness.

Bill had just been released from jail. He'd been arrested, in part, for his living arrangements; he'd built a makeshift camp within city limits, ignoring multiple police requests for him to pack up and leave. When he was released, we accompanied him back to the simple place in the woods he called "home." As we walked, he vowed to be more careful about his drinking, which had also been a factor in his incarceration.

Bill hunched over, limping, as we wound around bushes, avoiding branches in our path. His camp was just a short distance from a liquor store and fast-food restaurant, but if someone had not brought me here, I'd never have been able to locate it. His pace quickened, as did his speech. He was excited to soon be at "my place."

A peaceful creek ran parallel to railroad tracks just a few feet from his doorstep. Bill's "place" was a plastic abode below scruffy trees, wildly woven pieces of material held together with twine. He'd collected some metal, which provided additional structure to brace him from the elements. Rain was always the hardest, he said—and there were the snakes, insects, and the human predators from his village.

The wind had blown Bill's plastic, once attached to moss-covered tree limbs, into disarray. The site had been rummaged through, and his stained, now damp mattress rested at a sad angle. Only a few cheap pails of his possessions remained, the rest either removed by the police or stolen during the two-week chaos of his incarceration. His neighbors had known his life items were up for grabs.

He said, "I'll need to clean this up after I work my six hours." Bill had a temp job that would give him enough money for the next few days' binge of booze and smokes. "If I don't make enough, I will beg."

He mentioned this hadn't been his first trip to the slammer. I knew that after his last arrest the police would soon be back here, in his face, threatening him with another confinement if he didn't move on. Yet he wouldn't; this was his home.

I asked if he'd consider going to a shelter, and he mumbled no as he shrugged his shoulders. This had been the way he has lived for twenty years, existing the way he wished, and he didn't or couldn't change at this point, despite his difficulties with law enforcement.

He looked like he was sixty-five, but I was sure he was much younger than his weathered face and mental weariness made him appear. He had given up on life; I could see it in his face, the way he walked, and the way he talked. He was done, waiting for the inevitable as he swore at the police who kept harassing him.

Bill was the result of society trying to impose changes on unwilling, damaged, and depressed individuals, as the stress of daily life grows and they fail to comply. Sobriety, for Bill, was more painful than slipping into yet one more blissful, alcoholic escape.

Some sink so low that they no longer have the tools or energy to pull themselves out of this gully.

Unfortunately, major depression affects about 7 percent of the U.S. population at any given time, with 20–25 percent suffering an episode at some time in their life. Wounded people often look for a way to cope from all the stresses through drugs—either illicit or prescription—and alcohol. They need more of each drink or drug over time to raise their level of dopamine and produce the same good feelings to cope, resulting in an unending cycle. Long-term substance abuse may cause or worsen depressive symptoms.

I didn't see Bill being able to recover from his homelessness and surviving.

Brianna, thankfully, was in a better space, both physically and mentally. According to her, the mobile homeless are the fastest-growing homeless population. She seems to have no addictions and is willing to try alternative solutions to change. Appreciating what she has, she can rattle off a list of her assets, with the most important being her safety. She used to be disgusted by homelessness, but now, with her new lifestyle, she has become more open and considerate of others' issues. She attempts to live in the moment and adapt.

At a very young age, Brianna found her way by visualizing the world she wanted to live in and persisting with that image. She learned survival skills. Now she fights back from the effects of the physical, emotional, and sexual abuse she suffered from a parent and relative when she was growing up. She was a determined child, with her first job at ten years old. As a teen, she supported her mom and herself, even as she was occasionally kicked out of the house.

She talks about how she is amazed at some of the people she encounters who are homeless, but trying to blend in. There was a doctor and his wife, a man who speaks four languages, and another who owned multiple pieces of real estate. Each had their own story. They were laid off or for some reason lost a job; they expected to find the next work opportunity, but their unemployment and savings ran out. There were few options then, unless a generous relative or friend offered assistance. When that didn't happen, their homes were foreclosed on, and they were left to live with the only solution to survive — the streets.

Some people are homeless as a result of domestic violence. Women stay in bad situations owing to insufficient financial resources, fears, shame, or to protect their children. The abuse often causes physical disabilities, chronic health problems, mental illness, and PTSD, limiting later financial options when they do leave. They end up injured on the street after they finally give up trying to stay in wounding partnerships. The divorced, with few resources, often find their path to the cement. They are often hauling children, to boot.

In a *Huffington Post* article, I found a ray of hope — a story about a group of people working with the community of Cleveland's homeless families, hoping to reshape their lives and provide a path for their children. According to the article, one in thirty children was homeless in the U.S. in 2014. It asks why the American dream has disappeared.

The article outlined how a program called Project Love is changing the rules of the game for youths in inner-city, poverty-ridden areas. Kids need to believe to achieve. They want to survive. Yet a belief in self comes from having a life purpose with defined and visualized hopes and dreams. Project Love builds relationships of encouragement — to help kids graduate, get a job, or go to college. Teens learn how to behave in the workplace and how to interact with their mentors, which encourages their development. They receive the social and emotional support they need to "win" this game.

Brianna is steps beyond all that. It hasn't been easy. She thought her strategy was figured out, but suffered a setback when Walmart towed her home, after a conflict of priorities between a store manager, who told Brianna she could stay as long as she wished, and corporate interests. Brianna found a converted shed, which was her new home while she came to grips with the real world. She learned to be realistic. She was surrounded by others in makeshift arrangements—living in garages, sheds, even a converted bus. Together, they create a sense of community. When bureaucrats or law enforcement drop by, they clear out, but they always returned.

The latest information I found on her was that she was working as a marketing assistant for a nonprofit, but the salary was just not enough for her to afford an apartment close enough to her job or to pay both rent and gas prices for a long commute. Living just below the level where she can pull herself from homelessness, she keeps searching for the key. She says emphatically that she will work hard and someday will move on.

Looking back at where she was and is now, Brianna didn't feel prepared to take this all on. Who is? Maybe it's one reason we deposit money into savings accounts, relinquishing some pleasure now for our future safety net. But Brianna has also surprised herself in her agility to weather this storm, and in a strength she never suspected. She admits we all need the support of good people. More affordable housing could help, as would more government programs with work incentives.

Looking at the homeless, Brianna dismisses the stereotypes of *dirty*, *lazy*, or *ill*. "You can't survive being without a home or apartment and be lazy. It takes extreme effort to make it through each day. You don't have anything to eat, no way to get someplace to crash. You have to worry, plan, and figure that part out. Being depressed and exhausted takes its toll," she explains.

To manage her frustration, she started a blog about her experiences. Her following grew, and she was offered a part-time magazine internship. That developed into her first book, *The Girl's Guide to Homelessness*.

Working hard is usually not the answer. A support group of relatives and friends, a continued positive attitude, and maybe a bit of good old-fashioned luck could be her keys.

With goals and dreams pushing her forward, she advocates for homelessness.

An update on Brianna

Brianna is a cofounder of World Homeless Day, a grassroots global initiative that launched on 10/10/10 and has been recognized with yearly events in more than one hundred countries to raise awareness of the homeless and how we can help through fund-raising and education. She joined the Board of Directors for the California Coalition for Youth, which operates the California Youth Crisis Line and collaborates with the youth of California to participate in democracy and advocacy at a hands-on level.

12
Bridge Collapse

~

After considering the homeless encounters of Brianna's life, understanding a snippet from that time and her struggles, this next encounter with fate and possible death grabbed me. How can a person fight so furiously for life during crisis? Why does someone want to live despite all the signs that they can't? Is it possible, and if so, how?

~

ALICIA BABATZ WAS ON THE WAY TO PICK up her two-year-old daughter. The bridge she crossed daily suddenly felt strange. Was it an earthquake? Maybe her stomach was acting up? It was rush hour, and the bridge was crowded with vehicles. Yet there was a split, with gnarly edges, and then the whole bridge collapsed. Within seconds Alicia's car plunged down sixty feet into the Mississippi River.

The auto crashed through the concrete, then into the water, with Alicia still buckled behind the wheel. She watched the water around her filling the car as it started to sink.

It was the I-35W bridge collapse in Minneapolis, Minnesota, in 2007. The central span of concrete gave way, followed by the adjoining connectors. One hundred eleven vehicles and eighteen construction workers fell as far as 115 feet onto crumbling concrete and into murky water, where they struggled to stay alive.

The National Transportation Safety Board later decided that the probable cause was a design flaw in the structure.

Alicia's initial response was disbelief. "How could this be happening, and how could it be happening to me?"

she thought. Her car floated briefly in the water but soon sunk beneath the surface. She felt she would surely die.

Holding her breath underwater became harder, and she felt as if her lungs would soon collapse. Her mind urged her to take a gulp of whatever surrounded her, even if it wasn't air. Her thoughts raced, and she contemplated succumbing to her watery grave. She felt life, as she knew it, was over; she would certainly die. She accepted this, resigned herself peacefully to death, and just waited. Her body began to serenely float.

But *no*. Alicia was not dead. She realized she was still alive—barely, but still alive. Her thought process defied relinquishing her life and she decided to fight for a new breath, to fight for her life.

But how? She searched, calmly focused on finding that answer. She acknowledged that she was the only person who could help herself at this moment, so her efforts to escape multiplied despite unbearable pain.

Searching in the inky blackness for an escape, Alicia miraculously found the door handle, unbuckled her seat belt, and jerked with her whole being on the door that was the barrier to life. It opened. Again, with newfound strength and her will to live, she pushed out of the coffin and swam up toward the light at the water's surface. She erupted into the oxygen that could fill her starved lungs and took a gasp of blessed air.

It took her thirty minutes to get through the water and to where hands reached to rescue her, pulling her safely onshore. Her left shoulder was bruised from the seatbelt imprint and her body bleeding. Not able to focus in her numbed state, she wasn't even aware of the pain for some time, but knew she was one lucky girl to have made it to safety.

Alicia did many things right. After her initial shock and denial, she calmed herself. She was prepared to die, but as she looked at her death, she rejected it and fought to find her way out, remaining calm while she devised her plan. She refused to succumb.

She wasn't the only one caught on the bridge that day. As the connector twisted, swayed, and then the total span cracked, falling into the swiftly moving water, cars exploded like rockets into the air and fell like dominos, floating momentarily and then sinking to the river's bottom. Many people escaped, but thirteen didn't. Why?

What was the difference in the circumstances and spirits of those who lived? Maybe it was their defiance, their struggle not to resign or welcome death. Maybe it was something they remembered about what to do when a car is submerged in water.

Could it be as simple as a special amino acid in the brain that is dependent on fat and sugar to stimulate the release of neuropeptides, which affect the nervous system and lower stress and fear in some? Researchers conducted studies on Special Forces soldiers and how they handle stress and felt this could be a component of those who survive, the lucky ones?

Each story of someone involved in that collapse is different. Jeff Ringate, a construction worker on the bridge, thought of his family and the baby due in a month, as he fell through the collapsed structure. He landed on broken concrete and couldn't believe he was alive. He heard people below screaming for help. It was a living hell. Weeks later, he was still traumatized, not able to sleep well with the images and sounds stuck in his mind.

Thuy Vo also couldn't stop the nightmares, or the memories of what actually happened. Her car fell into the river, and she watched the water rise. She screamed, "Please help me! I don't know how to swim!" No one could reach her though, and she knew she must help herself. With a vision of survival, she took off her shoes, climbed out the window of the car, and tried to move her body forward in the water. She sank, her head submerged, but she told herself, "Stay calm. Do the best you can." Surfacing, she saw a wire resting on the water nearby, and she was able to pull herself to safety.

Most survivors sought therapy for PTSD. They found it helpful to share their experiences with other survivors from that fateful day. People in their everyday lives didn't get it. The progression of occurrences had been so unpredictable, that victims never knew what would happen next after the collapse started. That fear and uncertainty caused deep wounds.

Friends and relatives of those involved in the catastrophe suffered as well. Some lost loved ones, while others had to step in to help survivors deal with their pain.

Ben Hickman rushed to the hospital and recognized his unconscious wife's face. She was covered with debris from the collapse, wearing a neck brace, and breathing through a tube. Looking at her body, he cried in horror; her full, eight-month-pregnant belly was flat. The staff quickly showed him a picture of his newly born, healthy son. But it left an emotional mark.

Some relied on their faith. Lois Welman thought the shaking bridge was an earthquake, until she looked at her mirror and saw the man's face in the car behind her as he disappeared. The bridge collapsed directly in front and in back of her, and she screamed, "Help me, Jesus!" Her car fell but she crawled out alive, though she learned later that she suffered a compressed and fractured vertebra. She was happy to survive, yet she remembered how she felt going through the ordeal. She knew if it had to be, she would join the Lord. She felt her faith saw her through.

There are ultimate lessons learned from the bridge collapse. Stickney Ferguson realized her life could change in an instant, and she began to keep a journal to help her deal with the trauma. She was on a section of the bridge that only partially fell. Once out of her car, she panicked, fearing the pavement would collapse below her feet. A woman also trying to escape gallantly paused, helping Stickney over a barrier, and together the two souls, not knowing each other, became entwined in this event.

Stickney walked away from the smell of burning fuel, the sounds of sirens, and the workers who contributed to her safety. She became aware of the life experiences that shape who we are, help us make sense of our world, and show us how to live each day. Because life can change in an instant, she began to live with intention.

Many of the survivors who were interviewed after the event mention a renewed or new connection to a higher spirit and an awareness that we are not always in control. Fate, the spirits, decide what happens.

Emotional and physical survivors often become magnanimous with their fellow man. But they also assume the burden of *why*—why they lived and others on the bridge didn't. Survival is amazing, but often comes with a price.

After disasters, survivors have many emotions to work through. The first is denial, disbelief with accompanying shock. Eventually, if there is time, acceptance follows, and the person must devise a plan on how to proceed. Last, and most important, is action.

Garrett Ebling's auto also fell from the bridge into the water. Days earlier, he had proposed to his girlfriend, and he was excited about the life they would share. Then, returning from a company picnic and passing over the bridge, he suddenly felt weightless.

Garrett suffered a traumatic brain injury and was in a coma. Every facial bone plate shattered on impact with the water, a force that was comparable to hitting a brick wall at one hundred miles per hour. It was the worst injury doctors saw. They wired Garrett's mouth shut for healing. Tubes protruded from his stomach and neck. A cast covered his legs, and straps held his arms immobile. He lost many of his teeth and what remained were oddly reconfigured in his mouth.

A year later, he was pushing his limits, exceeding what his therapists thought possible. Outwardly, he made a remarkable recovery. Only his new wife, Sonja, guessed the depths of his depression.

He suffered from PTSD and struggled to recover for years. Each time reaching one milestone, Garrett expected to be *normal*. When he wasn't, his emotional injuries worsened; he felt numb and angry, jealous of others' lives. He became confrontational and controlling—if he couldn't control his own life, he'd control others. Sonja convinced him to challenge his anger in therapy.

Mad and agitated, he didn't want to face his feelings—but, remarkably, he did.

PTSD, in Garrett's case, robbed him of his core existence by creating new fears, rage, and feelings of loss. He was unable to control his domain; his lack of joy in life resulted in challenging relationships. His world was at a standstill, and he didn't know how to fix the emotional part, just wanting his previous life back.

In 2010, fighting his response to trauma and his anger, he finally discovered a solution for recovery.

God.

He asked God to take the reins and guide him to do the work.

As a survivor, Garrett has many of the qualities of a survivor—incredible strength, determination, and a positive attitude. To that list, I'd also add his acceptance of spiritual guidance, and his movement forward to full life reentry.

13

Woman's Struggle— Negev

~

*In this next chapter, luck is of little consequence. Will
to overcome is what matters. The issue affects another
part of our globe, and is one Americans have little
understanding of, but should. It is actually similar to
the challenges of survival women have encountered for
centuries. With my love of feminist issues, I gladly include
the battle of one woman from a Middle Eastern culture.*

*Although Israel tries to change this difficult situation,
more needs to be done. Women themselves will need to
rise and address a transformation to make an impact
that will affect their and their children's lives.*

~

Oppressed women still face discrimi-nation in society. In many places, they have little power to change these attitudes and actions in their culture, but a few emerging, brave people are trying.

Bedouin people are primarily nomadic desert dwellers of Arab ethnic decent. There are Bedouin settlements in many areas, including Egypt, Syria, Jordan, Saudi Arabia, Yemen, Iraq, Africa, and Israel. Women wear brightly colored, long dresses when they are inside, but when outside they must wear an abaya, a long coat, and/or a burqa to cover their body, head, and hair.

According to a Human Rights and Welfare research digest article written by consultant March M. Wells and titled "Bedouin Women in the Naqab, Israel: Ongoing Transformation," more than half of these tribal nomads were moved to towns in 1948, after Israel declared independence. The remainder lived in unrecognized, illegal desert areas under Israel's influence with no subsidy or support. Here, without access to electricity, sewage systems, or running water, they barely subsist in makeshift metal structures and tents. The government continues to corral them into urban areas where women are doubly ostracized, both by their status as females and by their ethnic origin. This creates a life of handicaps in gaining employment, education, and health care.

Traditionally, before resettlement, the Bedouin's society was patriarchal—men interacted with strangers, guarded the land, and made most of the family decisions. Women remained at home, with authority over agricultural and livestock activities.

By shifting the families to cities and peripheral settlements, Bedouin women's responsibilities have eroded, along with their power and financial stability. They no longer have control over an important part of their domain, and are left largely subservient to the men in their households. Bedouin women are traditionally not allowed to work or leave their homes, or to interact with men other than family members.

According to a 2010 journal article by Dr. *Abu-Qarn,* "*Determinants of Labor Force Participation of Arab Women in the Negev," The Robert H. Arnow Center for Bedouin Studies and Development* stated that, in 2007, only 11 percent of Negev Bedouin women were in the Israeli labor force. Lack of education was one reason. The expectation of women to not leave their homes or travel was another.

Bedouin girls, if they are allowed to go to school at all, drop out of school before high school graduation at a rate of 85 percent, compared to 71 percent for boys. Few females go on to higher education. Israeli high school classes are coeducational, which can be a major obstacle for traditional families, where some fathers do not want their daughters to interact with males from other tribes. There are few women teachers, which can also be an issue for Bedouin fathers, who have total authority over whether their girls remain in school. For more information on this, see my Research Notes at the end of this book.

When I met Masai tribesmen in Kenya and Tanzania, I saw the same patriarchal culture and separation of duties; their division of gender roles was similar to that of the Bedouin culture. Early in the 1990s, the governments in Tanzania and Kenya began encouraging the Masai to leave their traditional nomadic life, in which they seemed content, and resettle in cities. Lured with subsidy payments, many agreed to the radical life change. The Masai I spoke with, though, indicated that many of the relocated families had lost their souls and their sense of what was important. Many later turned their backs on the financial rewards, returning to the land they loved. If there's no passion for life, what remains important?

Under the direction of Oxfam (an international confederation of countries striving for solutions to global poverty and injustice, including global warming), some proponents suggest reversing these urbanization programs in Africa because of the Masai's ability to farm the deserts and scrublands that may influence climate change. The tribes also seem happier on the barren land they love. Do we actually help cultures when we dictate their lifestyles?

The Bedouin women's issues, in particular, grew more pressing after Israel forced their move to cities. Modernization, in combination with inadequate housing, exposed women to new health hazards in the form of chemicals, pesticides, and improperly disposed waste in the unrecognized villages. The polluting industries and power lines in or near even the sanctioned villages compromise the health of the women and families. Yet heath care is unavailable in these settlements, and most female residents lack transportation to the limited health care services offered in nearby towns.

Mental health care is even scarcer, despite high rates of depression and other mental illnesses among Bedouin women. Where care does exist, few women use it because of the cultural taboos of treatment and the stigmatization of mental illness that still prevails in Bedouin culture.

One positive sign of progress in this situation is the decreasing occurrence of female genital mutilation (FGM) or "Khitan" in the Negev culture. The majority of these Bedouin's live in Southern Israel and originated from tribes of the Arabian Desert, sheepherders from the seventeenth century. Some were farmers or slaves from Egypt and Syria. Their passage and establishment in Israel has always been fraught with turmoil and the women have an added mark that establishes them as women of their culture—FGM. It is the removal of some or all of the external and sometimes internal genitalia with a blade or razor, and is still a ritual in many parts of Africa, Asia, the Middle East, and other parts of the world. Some view it as genital circumcision.

Sometimes the surgical act is performed with no anesthesia. Depending on the culture, FGM happens any time between the days after a girl's birth to puberty. In the Negev settlements, women perform FGM on one another while male members are away. A number of women arrive at a girl's house; one woman covers the child's mouth while the others hold her down. FGM is generally accepted to be barbaric and sometimes life threatening, with the risk of the victim bleeding to death and experiencing later reproductive issues.

According to UNICF, there were 130 million instances of FGM, worldwide, in 2006. In 2014, the World Health Organization's estimate was up to 140 million in twenty-nine countries.

But as of 2009, Integrated Regional Information Networks report that Negev tribes no longer practice this custom. Since 1933, they say, six Bedouin tribes have made a remarkable change through education, nearly eliminating this practice.

Dr. Alex Rabinowit disagrees, and still sees FGM performed. In an article he shared on www.ynetnews.com, Rabinowit says that the number of female genital mutilations may have decreased, but the practice is still prevalent in some settlements, especially the unincorporated tribal Negev villages. "About ninety percent of the area's Bedouin women are circumcised," said a nurse at the Clalit Heath Services Clinic, who was fired after that statement.

A small ray of hope for Bedouin women in Israel comes from the Lakiya Weaving Center. The organization gives Bedouin women living in unrecognized areas employment and helps to keep their traditional crafts alive. I found similar weaving and artisan enterprises in Turkey during my travels. In both places, many mourn the slow death of traditional creative knowledge that is not being transferred to new generations. "There is little interest by the young, who focus on technological gadgets," a person explained to me in Turkey.

Domestic abuse also poses a genuine threat to the well-being of Bedouin women. The "Impact of High Fertility and Pervasive Domestic Violence" study reports that of two hundred Negev women interviewed, 48 percent reported violence, which caused poor mental health and gynecological problems. Domestic violence affected a large number of children as well.

The minimal availability of support services for these marginalized tribes means that few women receive assistance.

One of the key reasons for domestic abuse is gaining power and control in a relationship. Women stay in a bad situation because of insufficient financial resources, fear, and shame, to protect their children or because that kind of behavior is accepted in their society. Children who live in a household with violence show aggression from an early age that later may contribute to furthering the cycle of abuse when they become adults.

In the Amazon, I stayed in a small *mestizo* village, Atun Cocha, where Eleanor Smithwick, PhD, created the Peruvian Amazon Conservation organization to medically aid, educate, and teach self-sufficiency along with rain forest conservation. The Post Medica de PAC, under Smithwick's direction, has become the area's clinic, assisting fourteen villages.

Women in the Amazon have also shifted from being valued, respected partners in the tribal community to undervalued, voiceless domestic servants and reproductive slaves. Since the conquest of the *conquistadors*, women were totally subverted to men's expectations and needs. Today, women in some parts of the Amazon start having children at twelve or thirteen years old, and by twenty-five many have given birth five or six times, if they haven't died from postpartum hemorrhaging. Eleanor told me that often, husbands take additional, younger wives, leaving mothers and children without resources.

A major emphasis of Eleanor's clinic, besides treating the body, is providing emotional assistance to help women achieve financial independence and a way to be self-sufficient. Dr. Smithwick shares how small changes in sanitation, nutrition, first aid, and family planning can help Amazonian people live better lives.

She is helping these women survive.

In my first book, *Courage Quest*, there is a section on Peru, where you can read more about the wonderful services provided by the clinic and how Eleanor has helped change the life of women there.

But in Israel, one Negev Bedouin woman has learned another way to survive — through defiance.

Amal Elsana Alh'jooj was born in a small, unrecognized village without utility services. She quickly learned about the role of women in her community and in the larger country of Israel. She was the fifth daughter born to her parents. This was not a good thing in an Arab family. Amal's mother was shamed each time she delivered another female. She never said that to Amal, but the girl could see it in her actions. Her father could not go to some of the daily religious gatherings because he had no male children. As she grew, Amal took on this burden of her parents' shame and pain. She felt like her birth was a tragedy.

At five, Amal became the family shepherd. She left the house at five o'clock in the morning and returned from the hills when night fell. She was responsible for twenty sheep and additional animals.

But then things changed for her family. Their five girls were followed by five boys, born in a row. Amal now felt her inferior place at the dinner table, as her brothers were given chicken while she got none. They went to school, but her father pulled her out when she was just fourteen years old.

She now knew what it was to be a female in an Arab household.

Her grandmother taught her to always ask questions, to learn *why* and *how*. She told Amal to search for answers that would expand her life. She was emphatic that Amal never give up in life. These were the lessons that moved Amal forward to overcome.

One day, the Israel police arrived with demolition equipment and destroyed her grandma's home. "Why?" she asked, as she was taught. "Because it is in an unrecognized village."

Amal was angry at her status, something she had done nothing to earn, and frustrated with her inability to change others' perception of women. That anger moved her to a solution. At fourteen, she started to teach her own mother, and then most of the women in her community, how to read and write. She explained to those who questioned, "It is so they will be able to read the Qur'an." But Amal knew that they would soon also read a newspaper.

She became a female activist, who some would call a feminist, in an unlikely world of the lowest of lows in Israel. Amal's strength and will to overcome her status in birth and the recognition she received, elevated her struggle to not only survive but to thrive with her newfound passion for life.

Refusing to take the role of a victim or a second-class citizen, Amal pushed for equality. Her actions came with a price. Fear often ruled her life. Men tried to cause accidents; her car was set on fire. She received death threats.

Her persistence and a belief in her efforts to change the role of women in her culture and be accepted by Israelis led her to earn a master's degree and then a PhD. She received numerous awards, including a Nobel Peace Prize nomination and a New Israel Fund Human Rights Award. She's moved her causes ahead by being passionate, believing, as her grandma taught her, to never give up.

When she was in college, Amal met Israelis for the first time in a context that was not a negative experience. Previously, she only had contact with the Israeli police. She realized that before they could make things work in their bitterly divided country, people first needed to be proud of themselves. They needed self-confidence before they could lose their suspicion of others and accept other cultures' differences and uniqueness.

With this in mind, Amal started an elementary school with Arab and Israeli students combined in classes. She shows these young children how to live with no prejudices; it's a first step.

"You need to be part of the solution or you are part of the problem," she states.

YouTube link

For a link to a YouTube video about Amal's approach to unifying her country and elevating women's position in her society, see the My Research *section at the end of this book.*

14

Crash in Enemy Water

A woman struggles in Israel, making headway as she leaves the past behind and enters the future. Refusing to be a victim, she survives and grows, not only for herself, but for her sisters to join the world of today.

The men I will next tell you about fought desperately to live, as well. Their stories are about bravery, sacrifice, and maybe luck as they encounter the savage seas.

THIS IS A STORY OF COURAGE AND COM-
mitment—military style.

During the Cold War, the U.S. Navy flew regular mar-
itime patrol missions over the northern Pacific Ocean
between the Kamchatka Peninsula, part of the Soviet
Union, and the Aleutian Islands, which belonged to the
U.S. On October 26, 1978, Alfa Foxtrot 586, a P-3C anti-
submarine warfare aircraft, was flying a routine surveil-
lance mission over the cold waters in order to identify
and track Russian submarines. This was a constant cat-
and-mouse game of chase, so that if war actually broke
out between the two countries, the P-3 would be prepared to quickly attack and sink Russian submarines.

The four-engine turboprop aircraft had a crew of fifteen men.

Pilot Jerry Grigsby tried to steady his plane. Grigsby
had feathered (shut down) one engine to save fuel. When
he fired it back up, the flight engineer on board watched
the gauge of prop revolutions edging up to a dangerous
number. Grigsby engaged the emergency handle and the
engine cut, but the propeller did not stop.

Something was very wrong.

The propeller continued to malfunction, rotating faster
and faster regardless of what the crew did. If they could

not slow the revolutions, the propeller would eventually rip from the plane.

Grigsby's stellar training and composed nature showed. He increased altitude, hoping that would slow the propeller and resolve the issue. He tried everything he had learned, but to no avail. Their home base, ADAK Naval Air Station, was eight hundred miles away, so Grigsby changed course to Shemya, a closer land base but still 337 miles in the distance.

The propeller friction started an engine fire. Trained to counter numerous in-flight emergencies, including fire, the cockpit aircrew went through the emergency procedure, isolating and extinguishing the flames that were filling the cockpit with black smoke.

It was clear to Grigsby that a more radical decision would have to be made, and quickly. His actions would determine if his crew lived or died.

They weren't going to make it back to base. The only solution Grigsby saw was ditching the plane in the sea. Grigsby ordered his men to suit up with protective Cd-1 dry suits, which had tight rubber cuffs to keep water out, and don their life vests. He told them, "We're going to do what we are trained to do," and radioed their location as they descended.

Grigsby's military training guided his actions and assisted him in achieving what needed to be done, despite the stormy ocean. The courageous pilot guided his plane lower, slower, and closer to the water below. He landed as softly as possible, but one wing was still ripped from its body.

It was no easy landing, but owing to the pilot's exper-
tise, the P-3C hit the choppy seas, where the wind blew
at forty-three knots, safely, bouncing only a few times
while gliding on the upside of a trough between two big
waves. The engines exploded, and towers of steam rose
from the metal.

With the aircraft in the water, the evacuation and fight
for life began. One man either died on impact or was
unconscious and unable to exit the aircraft as it sank.
Another appeared to be trapped inside the downed plane;
the crew was unable to free him. But then, as if by a miracle, the fuselage rolled just slightly and lifted enough to
free his trapped leg and reveal a hatch. He dove out and
under the sinking plane and surfaced with the others.

The aircraft floated briefly as it filled with water, and
the men scrambled to inflate two rafts they had managed
to pull out from their plane before it sank, ninety seconds
after hitting the water.

Grigsby lingered behind, helping his men exit the
burning plane and making sure as many as possible
escaped. He followed them into the water but was unable
to get onto the lifeboats. He swam to the larger raft,
almost making it, but the crew didn't have oars on board
to steer or reach for him, and the waves rocked the raft
violently. Then he swam to the smaller raft and several
times came close to grasping the ropes his men threw
him. But finally, he disappeared beneath a wave, and was
never seen again.

Four men scrambled into the larger raft that could
accommodate twelve, and the remaining nine struggled

with the seas and then crowded onto the small raft, which was meant for only three. The horizontal rain and driving sleet spray chilled their bodies while the wind increased. The tiny raft had no protection from the elements. The larger raft had a tent enclosure for protection that the men zipped into position. They were warmer than those in the other raft as the temperatures decreased substantially after sunset.

Waves crashed on the men as they tried to steady the small boats and not flip. Water was rapidly filling up their life-saving enclosures, and they realized they were sinking. A valve in the boat had ruptured. They bailed, and with new conviction to live, they found the source of the leak, repaired it, and continued to bail as liquid poured from the angry clouds above and the cresting waves that crashed over the sides of the boat. They made little headway against the frigid water, which was already waist-high, numbing their limbs.

The waves were their most frightening enemy. The turbulent sea would raise the rafts twenty to thirty feet, then send them crashing down, almost flipping them. This happened two or three times every minute. Most of the men were violently seasick.

Their insulated survival suits offered some protection against the cold and rain, but they leaked and were not very effective. Only one aviator had gloves, none hoods. They were all freezing—freezing to their death.

Struggling for survival against the elements.

Three men in the small raft died of hypothermia, which can kill in many ways. As body temperature decreases, your sodium level plummets, you vomit (in this case, the violent motion of the seas also caused sickness), and dehydration occurs from the loss of electrolytes. Confusion, loss of energy, fatigue, muscle weakness, possible seizures, and coma follow, resulting in eventual death.

One of the men who died kept slipping and submerging himself in the icy water. His crewmates pulled him back out every time, but his heart, lungs, and chest were progressively chilled.

The men sang to build their morale and slapped each other's faces to stay awake, as sleep could be deadly. Their positive attitude is probably the most important factor that contributed to their survival.

Hope came when they saw a reconnaissance plane above. Before the crash, the crew had attempted to contact a U.S. ship just a few miles away, but the ship's radio was turned off. Other ships were not able to divert and assist because of the storm's hazardous conditions.

They had been found, but when no ship appeared, the survivors started to give up hope for a rescue. As darkness approached, they felt they couldn't be found in the night.

In the sky above them, Bill Porter, aircraft commander of a Coast Guard 1500 prop jet, was returning from patrolling the twenty-mile fishing limit between the countries. Although low on fuel, he received instructions to fly to the location of the downed plane. A Navy P-3C was tracking the life rafts, but needed to be relieved for its own low fuel level.

Before leaving the area, the P-3C climbed to two thousand feet to check its radar, and it located another ship just twenty-eight miles away. The copilot started transmitting on the marine band emergency frequency and was finally answered by a Soviet fishing vessel, the Sinyavin.

He relayed the plight of the downed plane. When the Soviets asked who was in the water, he said simply "friends," fearing the Soviets would not go to rescue Americans.

The reply was, "I understand," and the Sinyavin captain agreed to go and assist the downed crew.

The winds increased, visibility lowered, and squalls mounted. The boat could only move at ten knots. While they waited, every fifteen minutes Bill Porter dropped a smoke float to identify the rafts for the fishing craft.

The rescue ship arrived, shining lights onto the first raft. The men would live.

It wasn't easy in the choppy waves to move close to the life raft without crushing it, as the Americans bobbed like corks in the murky water. They made several attempts before they were able to connect, while the fishing boat acted like a shield to block the wind and cross waves. The Soviets lowered a thirty-foot, motorized whaling board. Lighter than the waterlogged raft, it rode higher in the waves and almost threw four of the survivors into the raging ocean. But finally, the Soviet fishermen raised each man to the boat deck.

In their numbed state, many of the airmen could not stand when brought on board the vessel. They had been so cramped after squatting in their raft for hours that they needed assistance just moving around.

When the crew was safe, the Soviets set out to search for the second craft, which had drifted two miles beyond. In the fog of night, it was not an easy task. But with the help of the strong searchlight, in thirty minutes they'd located the larger raft. Jubilant, the American crew knew their prayers were answered; they would see their families again.

The aircrew welcomed their saviors, who had swiftly, without questions and despite the treacherous seas, saved men from another country. Yet they were hesitant to admit their true reconnaissance operation to the Russians. It was so sensitive that thousands of miles away, the National Security Council and Departments of State and Defense in Washington had already been informed about the downed plane and the possibility of an international incident.

To the Americans' surprise, the Soviets did not detain the men. The fishermen welcomed them, covering them with heavy coats and giving them warm food, drink, and medical attention. They took them directly to a Russian port and then to an American hospital that eventually returned them to Moffett Field in the United States. The Russians risked their lives during this rescue of Americans.

This was a mission of people in distress aided by other people. Despite the politics of the time, it was just a fishing boat helping "friends" in the water.

This was the first time a plane had crashed into the icy Pacific waters and left survivors. Ten of the original crew returned.

The airmen's training, lifesaving technology, and an attitude of encouragement all contributed to their survival. The presence of the Coast Guard planes, which sustained hope, and pilot Grigsby's focused thinking were also key factors.

Ed Flow, on board the open raft, later commented that he never thought of succumbing to the elements. He was a fighter and believed he would survive. At the same time, considering the violent seas and freezing temperatures, he knew they would have died within a couple hours had they not been rescued when they were.

Grigsby's mother described her son's death this way: "Let me tell you a story about Jerry. Twenty-four years ago, when he was twelve, he almost drowned in a pool. We got him out and have had twenty-four good years of life with him, twenty-four years of helping him get ready for this moment when he had the opportunity to save the lives of others. We can't get too upset about that, can we?"

Jerry Grigsby was awarded the Distinguished Flying Cross, one of the military's highest peacetime medals, for extraordinary heroism and professionalism above and beyond the call of duty.

15

Canyon Runner

⮑

Some people are born with a stubborn persistence to overcome trials. They use their knowledge, learned from a lifetime of experience, and the training they receive along the way. Unsuspecting heroes save lives. The previous story demonstrated many of those aspects, as does the following struggle for survival.

⮑

YOU NEVER KNOW WHAT MIGHT GET YOU in life. One minute you are on top of the world, and then one false shoe plant can end it all.

One night, during a blizzard in my area, I wanted some diversion. I watched a documentary series, *I Shouldn't Be Alive*, which included a story about a canyon runner I decided to explore later.

Danelle Ballengee was a four-time, world-champion adventure racer who had already earned six "U.S. Athlete of the Year" titles. She set out one day on a normal, simple run in a Moab canyon. Tired and wanting to cut off some mileage, she drove past the popular lot where most people parked their cars and left her own car a bit farther up toward the trail.

Danelle was known for being a prepared person, and that day she grabbed a light fleece jacket to bring along, just in case. She was not a person who risked. However, she admitted later that she should not have gone five miles in without another person.

She ran with her three-year-old dog, Taz, a mutt Danelle rescued from the pound when he was three weeks old. They had an amazing, close relationship. At first, they took their normal path, but after a few miles they changed course, away from the much-traveled path and onto a Jeep trail where few explored.

She'd already drunk half her water when disaster struck. Danelle slipped on some ice and fell sixty feet down a canyon cliff, the equivalent of a six-story free fall. She landed on a remote ledge, with no people around.

Not realizing the full extent of her injuries, Danelle used her endurance training and moved ahead. Fit and intuitive, she thought she knew what to do. She quickly assessed herself and determined this was just a bad fall. She lay, prone, and knew she had broken bones, but she could feel both her legs, so she wasn't paralyzed. She would just have an inconvenient, painful walk back to her car.

Danelle planned to walk the thirty feet to the bottom of the canyon, over rocks and around bushes. If she couldn't walk, she'd crawl back three miles until someone saw her. It was only noon; she could make it to her car before dark.

In her fanny pack, she found two ibuprofen tablets and energy gel packets. She took the pills immediately to treat the agonizing pain.

Reality stuck when she realized she couldn't stand up. Her legs wouldn't move. She could only proceed by crawling, pulling each leg forward, one at a time, through sand and snow that covered scrub. Still, she started to move forward, dragging her injured body one inch at a time, scraping the desert floor. It took two-and-a-half hours to go the distance she'd run in minutes. It didn't matter; she kept her sights on each inch of progress, not on the long haul. By five o'clock, she had made one-quarter of a mile.

Her adrenaline surge helped in this desert crisis, as did her best friend, Taz.

With night approaching, Danelle realized she was in serious trouble. She was dressed in only the running clothes she'd considered sufficient in the day's warmth. Now her pelvis had split in two, leaving blood vessels damaged. The increasing cold shut off more blood supply to her extremities, the first state of hypothermia.

Danelle desperately tried not to sleep that night. She knew it would increase her hypothermia and could lead to death. She needed rest, wanted to sleep, but found ways to stay awake. She did crunches all night to stay warm, although she was only able to move her head and neck. She tapped her feet on a rock and rubbed her hands together to keep up circulation. She and Taz rested, curled up and touching; he provided warmth and companionship. Still, the hypothermia increased; she was losing her vision, and her body was shutting down.

The temperature dropped so much that in the morning, Danelle had to hit a puddle with a rock to break the ice and get her dog water. During the day, Taz would take off, then return to lick her face. His tail wagged as if he had been on a romp, but, later, Danelle realized he may have been searching for help to save her. Her dog was aware of her situation. I am not sure how, but he felt something was wrong, especially when Danelle could no longer move.

Taz helped raise her sprits and gave her something to live for. She watched an eagle in flight, the red rocks, the desert trees; she studied the environment and appreciated its beauty.

Fighting, but not losing hope, she was sure she'd survive. She felt an urgent desire to live. There were all the things she loved in life that she was not willing to relinquish. Her fight continued. Humans can endure more than they think, as long as they do not resign themselves to death.

Frustrated, she screamed in pain and in fear that no one would come and save her. Taz took off again. Was he looking for help, or was he afraid of the screams she couldn't stop. The dog eventually returned, but he refused to lay by her the second night. Her perceptions began changing.

Knowing that no one was aware of her location, Danelle desperately dragged her body two miles over rocks and through sandy loam, hoping to find a rescuer. The adrenaline was long since gone, and she was left to cope with excruciating pain, yet she surrendered to calm.

Dehydration set in; she didn't realize it at that time, but cold causes dehydration. Danelle saw a small puddle of muddy water and moved her body toward what could keep her alive. It took her two hours to reach the puddle and fill a water bottle, reaching behind her head because she could not turn her body.

Danelle was not aware of her life-threatening internal bleeding, although she knew that the lump she felt in her stomach wasn't good. There was a ball of clotting blood moving inside her. This additional loss of blood starved her brain. She got weaker and began to hallucinate. She saw strange images in the sky and heard bizarre voices that made no sense.

On that second evening, before nightfall, she told her dog she was hurt and told him to go for help. Taz tilted his head as if trying to understand. He stood, studying her, not moving. Then he raced away toward the canyon, and she was alone.

Taz returned, without help. Well, she reasoned, a dog doesn't understand English, does he? He still would not curl up next to her, but only put his paw on her stomach and licked her face. Was he recoiling because she was dying? Was a different scent emanating from her injured body that told him? Or did he realize where her pain was coming from?

I know for sure that dogs understand some of our language, and maybe some of our thoughts. They're definitely receptive to our emotions through a sixth sense. When my dog, Tasha, was near the end of her life, I experienced this, she sensed my concern. We were very close; I'd also raised her since a pup. She had come to my rescue before, including that day in the woods I wrote about earlier, and I'd learned to tune into her pain and her desires, as well.

Tasha let me know when she could no longer handle her discomfort and wished to die. I took her to her vet, who gently euthanized her. She died in my arms, and I felt the release of her spirit from her body in a breath of air that raised my hand from her chest. It sounds amazing, but there are so many things that humans usually aren't able to accept. We don't realize our animals' ability to transmit and receive messages.

During her racing career, Danelle was known for her endurance—for persevering through heat, cold, punishing climates, and geographies. She competed in races that stretched from one hour to ten days. But now, she had met her limit. Acknowledging that no one was coming for her, she knew she couldn't take much more.

Danelle had degrees in biology and kinesiology; she knew she was going to die in this beautiful spot. That knowledge gave her peace. She must leave this world. She reached acceptance.

But then she heard sounds. Again, Taz was off running. When he returned to his owner, he stopped to drink from the only puddle she could reach. She screamed at him for drinking *her* water, but she knew it wasn't her dog's fault. It wasn't anyone's.

She stopped tapping her feet, ready to relinquish her will and die, when she heard a voice telling her she must continue. Where was the voice coming from? She was alone, and she didn't believe in God. Yet it continued and would not stop. She saw strange stripes of white bands in the night sky.

Danelle did not really want to allow herself to die. She'd lose all the good things in her life—friends, families, and new future experiences. She wasn't ready for all of that to end, so she pleaded, screaming, for someone to realize she was missing and look for her. She tried to send a telepathic message to Dorothy, her nosy neighbor, willing her to notice that Danelle was missing. It was all she could do, and she had little hope this would help.

Why hadn't she told someone where she was going?

At daybreak on the third day, the annoying voices were gone, as were the stripes in the sky. The puddle water was again frozen, and with all her strength, Danelle broke the ice and drank, and then ate her last energy gel.

She possibly could move a few more feet forward. She debated. Was it worth the effort of a dying woman? Yes. Her persistence moved her forward. She would die trying.

She spent two hours going two feet forward, and then decided to return to the site of water. She had wasted her time and energy.

Drifting in and out of consciousness, Danelle again encouraged Taz to go for help. He whined, but reluctantly obeyed. She convinced herself to breathe slowly as she waited to die.

Danelle wasn't aware that the Grand County Search and Rescue Teams were searching for her.

Dorothy, her neighbor, had indeed noticed that Danelle's drapes weren't pulled, and that her computer and lights were left on, although her car was not in the driveway. On the second day that Taz didn't show up at Dorothy's doorstep for his customary biscuit, she became concerned and called Danelle's parents, who alerted the police.

A Moab detective, Craig Shumway, had a nagging feeling to follow up on a missing person, although the case officially had a low priority. Was it a hunch? Intuition? He drove out to check some running trails, something guiding him past the popular parking spot for hikers, beyond the farther area, where he found her truck.

Near the vehicle, running like crazy in circles, was Taz. The officer called to the dog but he would not come. First he dashed toward town, then returned and ran in the opposite direction. The rescuers tried to catch him, but he kept running away, so they decide to follow him.

One of the search-and-rescue volunteers, Bego Gerhart, chased Taz to the top of the hill. He doubted that anyone could live for so long in this December desert environment, but something pushed him forward with urgency, defying that logical feeling.

He found Danelle, alive, with Taz's head on her belly. Gerhard remarked how this dog was a hero, staying by her side through the ordeal.

Danelle and Gerhart both cried. Taz licked the rescuer, probably glad that his own mission was over and he could go back to being a normal, everyday dog.

Danelle was rushed to the hospital, and then airlifted to Denver, where she endured a six-hour surgery. She barely hung on, having lost one-third of her blood.

While she was still recovering in the hospital, she agreed to do an interview with *The Today Show* because they promised to include Taz. Danelle hadn't seen her dog, who was staying with her sister, Michelle, since her rescue. After the reunion and the interview, Michelle took Taz back home, but later realized he was missing. Sure enough, the dog showed up at Danelle's hospital. Now that's one special dog.

Was it luck that Danelle survived, or was it what we might call fate, possibly spiritual intervention?

Five years after her accident, *Runner's World* interviewed Danelle. She'd gone on to marry a man she met shortly before the accident, and the couple had two boys. She was happy and healthy, but said it had taken her four years to feel content with her life or to allow the emotions of the experience to surface and deal with them. She had nightmares for months.

Looking back at the experience, Danelle said her mind was in a different place during her crisis, which probably helped her survive. She mentions an increased awareness and feeling of spirituality. Maybe there is "something more" out there, she said. Many things just fell into place, and it couldn't just be pure luck. Either way, she shared her gratitude for her best bud, Taz, who gave her a second chance at life.

16

Antarctica Assaults

Danelle had a will to live; all of her efforts and previous training as a runner transferred to this desert ordeal.

These explorers who risk conquering new environments are also strong and committed, moving forward on the frozen ice with determination. The men in these next stories also had past experiences that assisted in their explorations.

The following stories were the most amazing quests I found when I set out to study those who pursued their desires. My research about these expeditions reveals significant reasons why some do and some do not survive. I've learned what drives men to take challenges, knowing the risks and possibility of death.

Their striving in the Antarctic fascinates, as do the contrasts of the different leaders' abilities, based on important decisions. Shackleton was a master of leadership, and even today, his name is used on a popular Outward Bound outdoor leadership program.

The other two stories are about men who were pragmatists, but took very different approaches to the tests they encountered.

Shackleton
Imperial Trans-Antarctic Expedition

Sir Ernest Shackleton was the leader of the Imperial Trans-Antarctic Expedition that took place between 1914 and 1916. It is an incredible story. Throughout his voyage, he was intently persistent, taking risks with a strong determination to complete his mission.

Those were three long years of constant challenges.

Shackleton was born in 1874. During his childhood, he was a voracious reader, and his favorite books, like mine, were those involving adventure. Bored with school and rejecting his father's desire that he study medicine, Shackleton left school when he was just sixteen and joined the crew of the Hoghton Tower, a ship bound for Valparaiso around Cape Horn. It was a harrowing adventure, filled with months of storms. They continued sailing to Chile and returned home one year later with barely enough food and water. Shackleton persisted, spending the next five years sailing to the Far East and America. At twenty-four, he became a ship commander.

Many successful people feel a similar wanderlust, seeing little value in formal education. When pursuing their own passions, they wildly flourish. Failure often touches their paths, but they continue and as their learning compounds, they eventually achieve their visualization. This was Shackleton's story.

During his career, he was a risk taker, investing in businesses in order to accumulate the wealth, security, and position he craved. That never materialized in his lifetime, and he remained badly in debt until his death. He tried his hand as a journalist and lecturer, but his love was the sea and the adventure of exploration, which fulfilled his life's meaning.

The Imperial Trans-Antarctic Expedition was his third attempt in Antarctica; he'd led two previous expeditions between 1901 and 1909. He considered his first trip with Robert Falcon Scott (the Scott of the famous polar region explorations and the Terra Nova discoveries) to be a personal failure. He embarked on an ambitious second attempt in 1907. In 1909, he made it to the farthest southern point in the world, near the South Pole, for which he was knighted by King Edward VII.

These experiences, along with his earlier experience sailing, helped to prepare him for his last adventure. He understood how to persevere through extreme conditions of cold with few resources. This time, his mission was scientific. He would sail the Weddell Sea — the stormiest, roughest body water in the world — and land a party in Vahsel Bay to cross, overland, the whole of Antarctica. The Ross Sea party would support them by traveling in the opposite direction and depositing a series of supplies along the final quarter of Shackleton's route.

Shackleton pursued financing for his venture ferociously, determined to get what he needed. When one avenue raised little, he went to the public, publishing the plan of his mission in a letter to the *London Times*. He solicited contributions from wealthy backers. He and his sponsors felt there was potential, if successful, for the Antarctic passage to make a profit. He persisted until all funds were raised.

Next, he recruited those who would take on Antarctica. The optimal window of time to leave for an adventure in the southern hemisphere was closing. He asked men—no females were accepted—to join an expedition that they may not return from, but if they did, their experience would generate recognition and success. Seamen would be paid $240, while scientists would make $750. He received five thousand responses to his appeal, including three from women who vowed, if necessary, to dress in men's clothes.

To choose the right men, he assessed character and temperament, not technical abilities. This became a major contributor to his mission's success, as the men worked well together as a team. With persistence, Shackleton had a twenty-eight-man crew before his deadline.

Shackleton sailed from Plymouth in August, 1914, on board his ship *The Endurance*. He arrived at St. Georgia, then departed December 5 for Vahsel Bay. However, in January ice packs surrounded his ship, trapping it and carrying them north. Shackleton had not expected ice during the spring and summer months.

For the expedition, they had brought sixty-nine dogs that were housed on the ship in small kennels along the port and starboard sides of the deck. They lived in cramped conditions, were exposed to nasty weather, and got tossed out of their kennels during rough weather.

The ship could not break free, constrained as it was like a moth in a web, and it was slowly crushed by the pressure of ice floes on its wooden structure. Mid-March, 1915, when it was obvious they would be caught in the ice for some time, the crew removed the sled dogs to provide the animals more protection and freedom to exercise. On the floating, frozen surface they established the dogs in ice kennels that they called "dogloos." The dogs

The Endurance shortly before its sinking.

were given sacks filled with straw, which they promptly tore to pieces in delight. Disaster was knocking, and after five weeks, Shackleton realized they would be trapped until spring. He ordered the crew to convert the ship to winter over.

Eight months later, in October 2015, the pressure of the ice was too much, and water began pouring into the ship. The crew pulled their personal possessions and survival gear and moved to an iceberg for safety. It took another month, but *The Endurance* eventually sank in the icy ocean.

Shackleton's crew spent two more months camping on floating ice, hoping it would drift toward Paulet Island, where they knew there was a food stash. As each ice floe broke, they moved to another, expecting that it would go the right direction. Instead, they drifted sixty miles from Paulet Island, and their concern increased.

While they were trapped for months on the ice near Elephant Island, Shackleton kept his men occupied with physical exercise, training, and an occasional concert performed with instruments they'd removed from the ship. They even played football with the dogs frequently interfering, to overcome the monotony of daily living.

With time, their shoes wore through; they had no replacements, so the men improvised and made new ones from wood salvaged from the broken ship. Every man but one suffered frostbite. How did he avoid it? He had a higher body temperature than most, but he also slept more than others, and often turned his bag inside out, shaking the frost that formed from his body heat condensation. He was vigilant in this pursuit, and he was rewarded.

With little of their original food left, the men resorted to hunting seals. One of the greatest dangers came from the killer whales that swam under the ice. The giant creatures would burst through the surface, breaking through the ice without warning to capture a seal. They left holes twenty-five feet in diameter, endangering the crew's lives.

The icebergs broke apart once again. Shackleton's men packed what they could into their small lifeboats and moved into any open water they could find among the ice floes. It was perilous, and their paths were erratic as the sea dragged them. For five days, they were often barely able to stay afloat. Constantly soaked by icy seawater, the crew deteriorated physically and mentally.

Shackleton calmly considered various scenarios and devised a forward action to bring them to the security of a stable land mass. His attributes of curiosity and openness to options made him able to adapt to his changing environment and find solutions to survive. He now had the challenge of his life, and adaptation was more important than the original plan.

They moved to the remote and uninhabited Elephant Island. After 497 days at sea, 346 miles from where *The Endurance* sank, they finally set foot on land. Relieved, they immediately erected their five tents.

Food was in short supply, but they subsisted on penguin, seal, fish, water, sugar, salt, biscuits, and hot tea in the evening.

At one point, Shackleton generously gave a sick crew member his daily biscuit ration. It was an empathetic act that the man never forgot. In *Points Unknown*, a sailor remarked, "That sacrifice will never leave me." Another time, Shackleton offered his mittens to a companion who'd lost his. In the ensuing months, Shackleton suffered frostbite. Yet in reward for his sacrifice, he received the complete devotion of his crew. They worked as a team out of respect for their popular leader.

With depleting supplies, Shackleton knew their best chance of survival, or maybe their only one, would be to take five of his men and go for help. They would sail to the South Georgia's whaling station, where he knew some of the villagers and trusted that help would be available to rescue the entire crew.

In a small, open boat, they rigged a canvas to provide shelter for men not on watch and protection from the huge waves and storms during their crossing. They loaded 250 pounds of ice for drinking water. The boat flipped when they launched it, submerging the sailors. There was no way to dry out, so they righted the craft and continued.

Shackleton instructed those remaining on Elephant Island to stay three more months, and if the rescue party did not return, to attempt to row to Deception Island. The men were physically weak and in bad condition. They decided to build a hut from the two remaining boats and scraps of their old tents. They stacked stone walls to support the structure, and added celluloid windows from a photographic case to finish off their digs. As the temperature rose, the snow melted, and the men had to bail hundreds of gallons of water from the bottom of their makeshift structure. When they ran out of food, they dug up seal bones and boiled them in salt water with kelp. The surgeon amputated one man's frostbitten toes. But they survived.

Shackleton and his crew made a harrowing, eight-hundred-mile trip in a boat just twenty feet long, through waters known to be the most storm swept in the world. They encountered icebergs the whole way that threatened to turn over their craft or crush them. In these tortured waters they kept a twenty-four-hour watch, and bailed a steady stream of liquid at their feet, the result of crashing, white-capped waves.

The men were constantly soaked with ice water that crested over the sides of their enclosure. Hurricane-force gales of more than sixty miles per hour continually blew them off course, and their boat became sluggish from the accumulating ice coating and moved more like a log.

These challenges were almost insurmountable. Several sleeping bags became soaked and then froze into forty-pound blocks of ice; those were thrown overboard. The men's legs chafed under wet clothing that had not been changed for months. Frostbite caused large blisters on fingers and hands. They were cramped in their sleeping quarters like spaghetti, never able to dry out.

The crew attempted to eat; they needed to consume four thousand calories per day to sustain their bodies from the difficult physical activities, but seasickness kept many of them from accomplishing this.

Shackleton accurately navigated this journey, so he would not overshoot the island. He used only a compass, charts, binoculars, and a sextant, which measured the distance of an object based on the angle of the horizon.

They could see their destination when they encountered the worst hurricane Shackleton had ever experienced. Just when they all thought that surely their lives would be lost to the sea, the wind shifted. A gap in a reef appeared, and they made it safely through the small entrance to a landing bay. Was this luck, providence, or just a deserved reward for their struggles? After a fifteen-day battle with the elements, suffering additional agonizing thirst for the last two days, Shackleton and his men landed safely on South Georgia, exhausted.

They were still seventeen miles from the Norwegian whaling village on this island. Shackleton took two men, leaving the rest onshore, and without a map, hiking gear, or skies, they embarked on a dangerous climb over snow-laden mountains and glaciers that no one had ever climbed, eventually reaching forty-five thousand feet in their search for a village.

On their thirty-two mile journey, they constantly retraced their steps, halted by impenetrable mountains and dangerous passes with crevasses. They had no camping gear, but used rocks for windbreaks, lining them with grass for warmth. They buried their cooker below the ground to allow a fire to start in the whipping wind. They never slept, which would be deadly, but instead kept each other awake.

Often they dug steps into the ice with a small tool. They moved constantly, never breaking except to eat, in the almost constant darkness of that time of the year. Once, the full moon appeared, and Shackleton felt it was their escort. He described a spiritual quality of guidance. The men saw it as a positive sign that their group would reunite. Spirits high, they even sang and laughed for the first time in months.

Then fog moved in from the ocean, making it impossible to see. They crept forward, hoping each move would not be their last. There was a faith among the men that something was guiding each boot plant. They eventually reached a precipice with a sheer drop down to the ocean, but they did not fall. Due to instinct or spiritual guidance, they were somehow aware not to take the step that would have ended their lives.

They needed to retrace once again and find a new path. Shackleton often queried his men on what the next move should be, involving his "team" in group decisions. At this juncture, the solution for an exhausted crew was not to backtrack, but to slide down the steep incline on their butts. Their pants were destroyed, but survival seemed imminent. In that moment, their joy and playfulness emerged as they all shouted like children and descended nine hundred feet in three minutes.

They were tired, hungry, and cold, but they could not give up, or all would be lost—their lives, the men waiting for them on the shore below, and their team on Elephant Island.

Finally, there was a gap in the ridge, and they went through. Huvik Harbor was five hundred feet straight below them, where villagers were going about their day's mission. They could walk five miles around to reach the whalers, or they could go down the precipice.

Shackleton queried his men. "Down the fastest way!" they all shouted. And so they rappelled straight down, roping and sliding five hundred vertical feet, eventually reaching a sandy beach after lowering each other down a waterfall of melting snow.

They reached the whaling station thirty-six hours after their trek began, two weeks from the start of the sailing voyage from Elephant Island that they had expected would take twice as long. The men were, finally, safe.

They found a boy who was shocked to see men who were not from his village, let alone men in their state. They were quite a sight, with long beards, matted hair, and tattered clothes that had not been washed in a year. The boy led them to the manager's house, where the explorers were welcomed and fed, and were soon planning the rescue of their crew.

Shackleton immediately organized a party to sail around the island to get the three men left onshore, and then set out for Elephant Island to retrieve the remaining crew. Near Elephant Island, sea ice surrounding the island turned them back four times. British and Chilean residents donated $2,263 for Shackleton to charter a schooner. The engine broke down, and finally the Chilean government loaned him a streamer.

After four and a half months, Shackleton finally spotted his men and shouted, "Are you all well?" Their reply was "All safe, all well." Reunited, the remaining twenty-two crew members traveled to Chile, where crowds welcomed them with admiration.

Shackleton survived the harshness of the arctic seas and floating ice walls in subzero temperatures, often soaked to the bone with seawater. Supplies and food were limited. Yet not one man was lost on the expedition. Shackleton saved his crew.

He never did complete the sea-to-sea Antarctica crossing. That feat was achieved forty years later by the Commonwealth Trans-Antarctic Expedition, but Shackleton laid the ground route that would avoid the Beardmore Glacier. He became recognized instead for his epic feat of endurance.

He attributed the success of his mission in part to the "providence" that guided him—a spirit or angels, he said.

During his many challenges and difficult decisions, he remained calm, reflective, and didn't panic. This enabled him to focus, weighing possible paths forward and then choosing what felt best. He definitely challenged life, as evidenced in his earlier pursuits, and he approached each in the spirit of courage as an adventurer.

Shackleton returned to the sea in 1921 to carry out scientific and survey activities, but he died of a heart attack.

Little attention was paid at the time of his return from his survival in extreme conditions of the Imperial Trans-Antarctic Expedition, but he was honored by the Royal Societies Club for his courage and endurance. One hundred years later, his accomplishments were rediscovered and recognized. Today, he has become a leadership role model.

An Outward Bound school in Boston displays the motto, "The journey is everything," modeled after Shackleton's leadership principles—bringing order from chaos, striving to make a positive difference in the world, and utilizing positive attitudes to accomplish goals.

"We had entered a year and a half before with well-found ship, full equipment, and high hopes. We had 'suffered, starved and triumphed, groveled down, yet grasped at glory, grown bigger in the bigness of the whole.' We had seen God in His splendors, heard the text that Nature renders. We had reached the naked souls of man."

— Sir Ernest Shackleton

This mission is certainly a testament to the fortitude and survival of sea warriors.

PBS reenactment of Shackleton's voyage

In 2013 a joint venture between Australia and the U.K. reenacted Shackleton's voyage and attempted to replicate his feat. They used a small boat built with the same materials to be the same size as the

*original, and ate the same rations. They wore comparable clothing
made from reindeer skins and waterproofed with wax, just as the crew
did; their conclusion was that wax just didn't work, they were constantly soaked, and they were amazed at how difficult their mission
was, while appreciating Shackleton's extreme efforts to accomplish his.
The PBS production was a Nova series called* Polar Expedition *and
can still be viewed. (See* My Research *for more information.)*

The Terra Nova Expedition

Two scientific expeditions set out in Antarctica just
before Shackleton's. Apsley Cherry-Garrard's men had a
will to live. They fought for their lives with optimism and
ingenuity. Robert Falcon Scott's team did not have those
resources for survival. Cherry-Garrard's mission was con-
siderably shorter in duration than Scott's, as well, but his
spirit was much more positive.

Both teams bravely set out, and each leader had previous experience exploring this tumultuous part of the
world, so they knew the risks.

Apsley Cherry-Garrard grew up hearing the stories of
his father's achievements in India and China, where he
fought for the British Defense Forces. The son strove to
live up to the father's example. After inheriting his family's sizable estate, he started to plan his own exploration
of the Antarctic.

At twenty-four he actively pursued a position in Robert Scott's expedition, but was turned down due to his
lack of experience. Craving to travel the world and face

dangers, he was not content to live the life of a wealthy gentleman, and he donated money to the expedition. He was then accepted as a crew member with the title of assistant zoologist, and he became the only man on the voyage with a college degree.

Cherry-Garrard was a sensitive, quiet, loyal gentleman. During the exploration, he proved his courage and ability to deal with pressure and move forward in crisis. He was also a charismatic, likeable, supportive chap who had the ability to understand what motivated the decisions of the men around him.

Between January and March 1911, Cherry-Garrard helped lay the supply depots in advance of Robert Scott's arctic expedition. He then accompanied Scott that November on his quest to be the first man to reach the South Pole. Along the journey, exhausted horses were shot and saved for food, and the dogs sent back to base camp.

In January 1912, Scott directed most of his support crew back to their base camp. He asked Cherry-Garrard to wait there until Scott reached the South Pole, and then to bring the sled dogs to assist his return.

While waiting for Scott, Cherry-Garrard and two friends made a separate scientific sled journey to obtain penguin eggs. They wanted to test a theory that penguin embryos were the most primitive on earth, still in an early stage of evolution. They tackled this mission during the coldest, darkest months of the year in the polar region. Birdie, one of the men in the party, hauled 750 pounds of equipment through the ice and snow in search of their goal.

Although Cherry-Garrard described it as the worst journey in the world, his charm and enthusiasm guided them as they sledded sixty miles at a time through blizzards, huddled in icy sleeping bags, and sang hymns to stay warm in the frigid temperatures, which reached 76 below zero.

They took meticulous, daily care to protect their feet and hands, often padding them with whatever was available, aware of what dangers lay ahead if frostbite set in. They attempted to eat a diet of hot, fatty foods. But still, all of Cherry-Garrard's teeth split into pieces from the constant chattering, and his dental nerves died.

Between hurricanes, the temperatures warmed to just twenty below, which seemed balmy. But then the wind started whipping with an indescribable fury, and the top of their igloo blew off. Gear blew away and shattered in the storm. Reclaiming their remaining possessions after it was over, Cherry-Garrard said only that it was the most wonderful thing to still have something, and they gave thanks.

Cherry-Garrard often referenced God in a positive way, as a force who was directing their future.

One blizzard tore away their tent and left them protected by only their sleeping bags, covered by snow drifts in the subzero temperatures for two days without food. They again sang, prayed, and hit each other; it was the only way to know, in the slashing snow and darkness, that the others were alive.

The group remained positive, planning their future moves despite losing their precious tent. They dug a hole in the ground, covered it with the tent floor cloth that remained, and got in their sleeping bags. They did not focus on negativity, the past, or possible death, but instead looked to the future and lived in the now.

They traveled nineteen days, arriving at Cape Crozier in mid-July. Cherry-Garrard's thoughts now focused on death. It had been a long, arduous journey, and he was weak, hungry, and depressed.

The men could no longer stand the extreme cold and exposure to the elements, but as they ventured forward, surprisingly, they discovered their canvas enclosure. The gale had blown the tent nine hundred feet down a cliff, but, miraculously, the zipper caught on a bamboo pole, keeping it from blowing into the sea. They were able to recover it. Hope once again became their mantra.

From that time forward, each night one person tied a rope around the zipper of the closed tent door and wrapped it around himself after he crawled into his sleeping bag. If the tent were to go, so would he.

Cherry-Garrard stated that the day's marches were bliss compared to night's rest; both were awful, but with a tent he now felt they would pull through. He described his men as self-sacrificing and courageous, standing every test. Even during their worst times, the men remained decent and civilized, using respectful words like "please" and "thank you," never swearing.

Feeling homesick and weak, they slept little and often stumbled into one another while falling asleep on their walks. Their toes were numb and frostbite was starting to show its effects. Birdie, one of the teammates, was the only one to never get frostbite. His sleeping bag fit the best, so he was able to ward it off.

Wilson, another team member, announced he was ready to return to the ship. The men were becoming callous as their memories blurred. They had come seventy miles in three weeks, at the height of winter; they all agreed to return, and so seventy miles back it would be.

They were done. Near the trip's end, Cherry-Garrard, weak and beaten, turned to death once again, stating, "I might have speculated on my chances of going to Heaven; candidly I did not care. I could not have wept if I had tried. I had no wish to review the evils of my past. But the past did seem to have been a waste. The road to Hell may be paved with good intentions: the road to Heaven is paved with lost opportunities."

He wanted to live his life over and spend his young years in a more meaningful way. He still desired a future, but in his weak, hungry state, he just crawled into his bag to stay warm and thought he might take morphine to end it.

All the team members' thoughts turned to death. The men did not fear it, although they feared the pain of dying. They all gave up. But as the temperature rose in their bags, they became comfortable and fell asleep. Upon waking, all their challenges looked better, and their will to live emerged.

Their outlooks improved as their wills to live surfaced. They fought for their lives at that point, using optimism and ingenuity to make do with whatever they had for their survival.

This idea amazes me. Just think how much can change if we only wait eight hours, and how different our obstacles and pain of life might appear. I learned this from my mom's story, through her desire to die when her health was at its worse and then how her outlook improved with her physical state.

Cherry-Garrard barely made it back to the base camp, but he recovered in time to strike out to meet Scott at One Ton Depot. He waited for seven days for Scott to arrive, but then left for home base. His dogs had no food, and one of his men was ill. Cherry-Garrard never forgave himself for what happened to Scott. When he returned home to England, he became bedridden, struggled with bouts of PTSD, and was never the same.

~

Robert Falcon Scott led two arctic missions. The first was his Discover Expedition, a scientific journey that lasted from 1901 to 1904, and the second was the Terra Nova Expedition that began in 1910 and lasted until 1913.

Captain Scott was a British naval officer who, in his early military career, drew the attention of the Secretary of the Royal Geographical Society. Clements Markham noted Scott's intelligence, enthusiasm, and charm. He marked the eighteen-year-old midshipman as a possible recruit for a future polar exploration.

Since his father had died, Scott was the sole supporter of his family, and these responsibilities must have driven his career. He actively pursued commissions. He volunteered for, and was awarded command of, the Discovery Expedition in 1901, which led to his discovery of the Polar Plateau.

His second exploration, the Terra Nova Expedition, began in 1910 and spanned three years. The operation was both scientific and exploratory, and Scott uncovered plant fossils that proved Antarctica was once forested and connected to other continents. But his actual passion during this mission was land discovery. He wanted to be the first man to reach the South Pole. For his efforts he became a British hero with many permanent memorials erected to recognize his bravery and his unwavering commitment to move forward and to conquer.

Scott and his fifty-man crew had little or no experience with the equipment that they took to Antarctica, especially the skis. Markham, however, considered specific skills less important than aptitude, so he chose Scott for his persistence. They did not know how to train the dogs that were on board his ship, and preferred man-hauling (human-pulled sleds).

During the first year of the Discovery Exploration, Scott traveled within 530 miles of the pole before he physically collapsed and had to abandon the venture. The next year his techniques improved, and he moved forward, continuing the Polar Plateau expedition.

Friction existed between Scott and Ernest Shackleton. Scott was not happy when, in 1909, Shackleton announced plans for his own challenge for the South Pole bid. Scott claimed he was the first to request a mission to discover this territory and Shackleton should not compete with him. Shackleton persisted until the British polar establishment rebuked him.

Organizing his new mission, Scott decided to use dogs, ponies, and a new, motorized sledge on the early portion of his trip, and then to rely on man-haul sledges in the latter stages, near the glaciers.

Learning of Scott's mission, Roald Amundsen, the Norwegian explorer, hurriedly prepared and set out on June 10, 1910, for his own adventure to Antarctica, making his base in the Bay of Whales. He, too, wanted to be the first man to the South Pole, so that he could claim it for Norway. He kept this objective a secret, even from his crew of four men, until they had boarded the ship.

En route to Antarctica, Scott received a telegram from Amundsen, telling him that he was tackling the South Pole with a goal to be first there. This motivated Scott forward, but his ship was trapped in ice and sank, so his quest was again delayed.

Amundsen's preparation took months. He had to lay his depots, and he suffered a false start that almost ended in disaster. He set out again in October 1911, and this time successfully planted his flag at the South Pole on December 14, 1911, using skis and sled dogs to move quickly across the unknown territory. He was probably also assisted by the knowledge he gained from previous starts, where he learned about the challenges he would face.

Scott's team finally left on November 1, 1911, for the pole. As they moved toward their objective, the man in charge of the ponies suggested Scott kill them for food. Two ponies had already died when they fell through the ice as the crew disembarked the ship; killer whales had attacked and ate them. Scott refused to kill the rest, but four ponies died during the journey anyway, either from the cold or when they slowed down the advance and had to be shot.

Scott and his team arrived at the South Pole on January 17, 1912, and realized that Amundsen had beaten him there by five weeks. Seeing the Norwegian flag planted where they'd visualized the British flag depressed the team. They never were able to rise above this disappointment. Scott's dream was gone. It became a major obstacle to their expedition.

All they could do now was retreat eight hundred miles back to the ship that would take them home, defeated. On January 19, they started their return journey. By February 7, they'd traveled three hundred miles. But then the hurricanes, snow drifts, and whirling flakes surrounded them.

Scott's team suffered a shortage of food and fuel. Their depots contained less than they expected. What had gone wrong?

At that point, frostbitten and unable to stay dry, the lack of food and heat left the team weakened and barely able to continue. They spent days battling horrific conditions, with colder temperatures and stronger winds than they prepared for. The weather was exceptionally bad even for this arctic region. Sand snow the size or corn kernels made travel difficult as they dragged their sleds. The men expected their homemade sails to catch winds to aid them across the surface, but the wind did not cooperate at this time. They slept little.

Scott was an unusually emotional person—maybe a bit of a depressed person. Cherry-Garrard wrote later that Scott exhibited major mood swings that could last for weeks. This didn't help with his expedition challenges.

One of the men, Edgar Evan, fell at the Beardmore Glacier, which left him "dull and incapable." He eventually died. Another man, Titus Oates, suffered invasive gangrene. Both situations substantially slowed the party's progress, but Scott refused to leave them to die alone. They just fell further behind their schedule.

Oates never complained as his body was consumed by the infection. In the end, knowing the burden he added to his team, he announced he was going for a long walk and disappeared into the snow. He was never seen again. It was a blessing to the men and a courageous act from a man who, though barely able to walk, walked to death.

An entry in Scott's diary reads, "The worst has happened." But also, "All the day dreams must go." He concludes, "Great God! This is an awful place."

Scott had left orders that his support party, which was confused by location and responsible parties, then eventually led by Cherry-Garrard, to take the dog teams south to meet them at One Ton Depot in early March and assist their return journey to the ship. There was only a short window of time left for sailing before winter season struck Antarctica.

In February 1912, Cherry-Garrard and dog handler, Dimitri Gerov, had set off from the ship, and they reached the rendezvous spot on March 3. They deposited additional food and waited there seven days, hoping to meet the South Pole team. Cherry-Garrard and Dimitri turned back on March 10, not believing Scott was coming. Scott's party, at that time, was a mere sixty miles away.

Scott talked about how "Providence is our aid," but on March 4 his meticulous diary revealed that he knew his end was near. There needed to be action, but they could not move through the continuing blizzard. He stated that each man, in his weakened state, must help themselves and not the others.

On March 12, resigned to their end but still fighting the good battle, the team talked about a way to make their deaths more comfortable. These men, just as Cherry-Garrard's men, were also not as fearful of death as they were of the pain of dying. There was enough morphine and opium in their medicine cabinet to do the job.

Yet no one used the drugs. They decided to die on their feet, moving forward toward the ship that was soon to leave, long past the time they planned to be on this inhospitable land mass. When the blizzard finally let up ten days later, they tried to walk, but by then they were all too weak. They returned to their tent to die.

In a farewell letter to Sir Edgar Speyer, dated March 16, Scott wrote, "We very nearly came through, and it's a pity to have missed it, but lately I have felt that we have overshot our mark. No one is to blame and I hope no attempt will be made to suggest that we had lacked support."

They were just eleven miles from One Ton Depot, where Cherry-Garrard left supplies weeks earlier.

Scott's diary describes his last two weeks of continuous storms. The men were confined in their tent, with only enough fuel to make two cups of tea each day.

"We took risks," he wrote, "we knew we took them; things have come out against us, and therefore we have no cause for complaint, but bow to the will of Providence, determined still to do our best to the last." He also wrote in his last days that he did not regret his journey, which showed that Englishmen can endure hardships, help one another, and meet death with as great fortitude as ever in the past. He stated that he was aware of the risks he took and knowingly accepted, and that if he had lived, he would have told the tale of the endurance and courage of his companions.

The man, pushed to the brink of his physical and emotional will, wrote his final diary entry on March 29: "Last entry. For God's sake, look after our people."

Cherry-Garrard returned the following arctic summer and found their bodies. Scott's team was still carrying thirty pounds of geological samples, as if they were precious stones, to bring back to the U.K. Here was a scientific search gone wrong. Cherry-Garrard was distraught and returned to England suffering from the loss.

Scott erred in several ways, or maybe he suffered what we call "bad luck." He brought only four pairs of skis for the five-man team, relied on man-hauling sledges instead of dogs, and he probably misjudged the potential severity of storms with winter approaching. Scott had pioneered motorized sledges, but issues prevented him from using them. Once the ponies died and the dog teams were sent back, it was just the men in harnesses, pulling their sledges.

Their failed mission possibly owed to bad planning, emotional degradation, and natural forces that intervened stopping forward movement, but God bless their spirits that pushed them to the bitter end. Today, the scientific base at the South Pole is inscribed with both Amundsen's and Scott's name.

Two of the men who died had previously survived an excursion with Cherry-Garrard just months earlier. Why do some keep striving for new adventures despite their knowledge of the risks? Is this courage or a desire for one more adventure?

Public perceptions of Scott have varied greatly over the years, swinging from hero to flawed leader. He was initially celebrated in Britain as a national icon, selfless and courageous. I believe he was.

All of these Antarctic stories demonstrate man's determination and bravery in exploration. Two succeeded, while the other lost. What were the characteristics of the leaders? Was foresight in planning the ultimate reason for the survival or loss? Do men succeed on guts alone, or is there more involved in survival?

These men in my Antarctica stories were all risk takers, but only Cherry-Garrard and Shackleton survived. The similarities of the winners are interesting. All the adventurers left school early and craved the extraordinary, to pave a new path. They were good leaders, building on morals and motivation. They improvised in the face of disaster, not sticking to a plan, and were open to new ways of doing things. They had a faith in providence, in a spirit beyond themselves. They felt guided.

Scott's expedition was pretty amazing from my standpoint. Religiously keeping a diary, he recorded the horrors of the deterioration he and his men endured. Outwardly, they appeared jovial in order to boost each other's morale, but inwardly they were probably all depressed, realizing they had not achieved the South Pole goal and battling the unending, monotonous days. Scott often wrote in his diary of being in that horrible place to labor without a reward. With no enthusiasm during their struggle, they lost faith, but they were men of stature and striving to achieve in difficult conditions.

Learning from the Master of Yukon Quest

Frank Turner with a Yukon Quest dog

People use different techniques to survive. Their goals may be different, but, above all, they must have the motivation to win. Here is a man who understood how to motivate animals to reach his goals — and he uses that to win time after time.

Frank Turner, who has raced in twenty-four Yukon Quests, offers a camp called Muktuk Adventures to train novice mushers (dog-sled drivers) and to mentor experienced ones. Frank also raises funds for the Disabilities Association of the Yukon. An explorer by heart, he has gone on a Siberian expedition and additional Arctic trips through the years.

ON A TRIP THROUGH ALASKA AND THE
Yukon, I stopped in the town of Whitehorse, where the
international dogsled race called the Yukon Quest happens every February. While there, I had the privilege
to meet Frank Turner, a winner and twenty-four-time
participant in the grassroots event, which is generally
accepted to be much more challenging than the better-
known Iditarod.

The Quest course is one thousand miles long, winding
from Whitehorse to Fairbanks along an old sled trail that
was used by gold seekers and postal carriers. It crosses frozen rivers, four mountain ranges, and isolated territories
full of moose and wolves. Participants complete it in ten
to twenty days. The weather brings additional surprises
each year—ice, river overflows, open water, whiteouts,
excessive wind, and cold. It's one tough race.

The entry fee is $1,500, and participants come from
all professions. Frank has raced against cabdrivers, swim
instructors, coal miners, tax collectors, lawyers, and trap-
pers, to name only some. Both men and women show
up to challenge their self-sufficiency and wilderness skills,
which is at the foundation of arctic survival. They all have
that can-do attitude and a strong desire to win. Temperatures can drop to sixty below, with a wind chill that will

take it to one hundred below. The wind blows up to fifty miles per hour in blizzard conditions.

Each musher begins with fourteen highly trained dogs. The preferred breeds are Alaskan Huskies and Siberians Huskies. Alaskans are larger and slower, but can pull more weight than the smaller Siberians. The competitors must, at all times, treat their dogs humanely; there are multiple checkpoints along the trail where veterinarians ensure the dogs are in good condition to continue racing; offenders are eliminated from the race. Each team must finish with at least six dogs.

Keeping in spirit with the Alaskan code of living, competitors must pack all of the food and provisions for both musher and animals, with a total weight not to exceed 250 pounds on their sleds. Before the race, they deposit additional food supplies at various locations along the route; it would be impossible to carry everything they need.

I got to spend two days on Frank's ranch in 2006, learning how he motivates and cares for his dogs. I wanted to know why he was a consistent survivor of one of the most difficult sled races in the world.

Frank was a short, fifty-eight year old man, with a slight paunch, graying beard, and wire-rim glasses that slid down over his nose. There was a twinkle in his eye, a bit like Santa. His thinning, curly hair barely swept his shoulders, poking out from his baseball cap.

It was not the appearance I expected from a champion, a person with enough gumption to consistently challenge the wilderness year after year. Yet at the time we met, he was the only contestant to have competed in every Quest, and he'd won numerous awards. What drives a man to do this?

Frank lived in Toronto before migrating west and settling in the Yukon. His career in Social Services brought him to the Selkirk First Nation—the unified group of Alaskan tribes that banded together in the early 1990s to garner clout and government support. Frank desired to help trace the native people's heritage and to develop pride in their ancestry as they shared their story with the world.

Frank eventually retired, and is now a free spirit pursuing his love of dogs and sledding.

He started racing in the first Yukon Quest in 1984, finishing fourteenth. In 1995, he set a record for the fastest time, completing the course in ten days, sixteen hours, twenty minutes. His record stood until 2010, when Hans Gatt completed the course in nine days, two hours. Frank has crossed the finish line seventeen times and has placed ten times in the top six.

When he won the Yukon Quest, Frank vowed to the press that this would be his last race.

Of course, it was not.

He opened his kennel and his training program for future racers to the public, offering tours. Guests find that Frank is a highly inspiring motivator. His stories and experiences create a spirit of courage, while challenging others to higher goals.

He explained to me how he racked up so many victories as he competed so often in the race. He said he never put up a tent for warmth, despite the subzero temperatures. When he stopped at night, he first cared for his animals, putting down hay for their warmth, mixing a hot dinner for them, then taking off their running boots. He would massage the dogs' bodies and paws, fix any damaged equipment, and consider strategizes for the next day's encounters.

Finally, it was his turn. He would eat and then go to sleep on top of his sleigh, with no blankets. He did this to stay tough, to not get comfortable. The unbelievable cold kept him alert and didn't allow him to rest long.

A typical musher in the Yukon Quest gets only a fraction of the sleep their animals do. Dogs may rest ten hours a day, but after settling camp and taking care of all the animals, the person may nap only seventy-five minutes. Mushers have suffered sleep deprivation, hallucinations, hypothermia, and frozen toes and fingers, which can be life threatening on the trail. Competitors become overwhelmed by pessimism and make poor decisions because of the sleep deprivation, which often results in losing the race. Frank, however, seemed to remain optimistic.

He's tough. In 2005, near the end of a race, he experienced incredible tooth pain. When he stopped, he insisted that the medical staff pull the broken tooth right there, without medication, so that he wouldn't miss out on the celebratory meal of ribs at the finish line. It was the third tooth he broke on the trail, eating his main meal of granola bars.

Frank chose dogs for each year's team based on specific qualities that would complement the total effort. He usually picked four females and ten males. He told me that the females were better at focusing and assessing the total challenge, while the males had more strength. It was worth losing some power to balance the group with the female qualities.

He rotated the dogs' positions within the pack, depending on each animal's individual strengths and what Frank needed at various times during the race.

He told me about a particular two-year-old male that he'd been watching all year as a possible lead. Other people would give up on this particular dog for this position, but Frank had seen a dog blossom into strength at as old as four years; it might have to do with the loss of shyness as the dog matured, he speculated.

If he saw a dog actively pursuing the lead, Frank would award him with it, and in return he was often rewarded with a winning effort.

Most of the dogs at the kennel got to run and play off leash while Frank chose a small group to pull aside for training. He lavished individual attention on each in a way that complemented the animal. "Play is important; it cannot just be work," he said with a smile as he lovingly rubbed the neck of a dog and praised him. Frank won the Vet's Choice Award twice for his exceptional care of his dogs in the Yukon Quest.

From the dogs' perspective, Frank was their leader, the alpha of the group, and they offered him their complete trust and respect; that's what made his team work. They felt he had their best interest at heart. That loyalty, in turn, ensured his survival in the remote terrain during the long days on the trail.

Frank told me that it was his dogs that won that 1995 race; his team taught him what he needed to do. He also learned to never underestimate his own potential. When I asked why he raced, he told me that he was addicted to it. This was his passion. Winning was the icing on the cake, but the cake was being out there with his dogs.

In 2007, he scratched the race for the first time, pulling out just eight hundred miles from the end. The course had been overworked, and for the dogs it was like running on pavement. He decided it was too much pounding for his animals. He said, "The only reason to go on would be to satisfy others' expectations, and that's not a good enough reason. You want to run a good race, but not at the expense of injury."

The competition with other racers was not what produced the best race for Frank. He just loved running with his dogs.

As I considered how to survive from a musher's experience, I watched how Frank worked with his dogs to create wins during his Quest races. What I saw were management skills and approaches that could be transferred to the business world.

Frank's relationships with his most valuable asset, his animals, allowed him to survive and win in the Yukon Quest against much younger contenders. He trained, nurtured, and conditioned his animals with positive reinforcement. In response, they offered extreme love and devotion to him.

Frank found fulfillment in his environment—nature, the outdoors, and his animals. In this space, he found his reward and felt whole.

When he started mushing in the mid-seventies, he tried to embrace the macho treatment of animals demonstrated by those who taught him. It seemed too harsh for him, and soon he shifted his philosophy from discipline to motivation. He started to watch women mushers who enjoyed themselves and their animals, and who pursued team management. They profoundly influenced Frank's style, shaping his perspective of the sport and training. He began to use constant rewards and rarely disciplined his animals. His motto became *a happy dog first, well-conditioned second*.

Frank's dogs lived in individual enclosures, tethered in closed pens with floors and roofs. However, sled dogs are pack animals, so he also ensured that each dog could reach at least two others to play.

He fed them well with vitamins, minerals, kokoheart coconut oil, bee pollen, and fatty snacks. Sometimes, in the winter, he treated them to bison heart, bison tongue, and other ingredients. As much as he could, he made sure they had the best.

On some training days, if the dogs didn't seem like they were enjoying the sledding, he'd comply and bring them home early. They would try again in a day or two. After all, aren't we all like that, with some days when we're off?

Dogs were chosen who had a good temperament; he didn't look for a record-of-winning pedigree. He wanted mental and emotional attributes of enthusiasm, gentleness, and a strong work ethic. I believe that matched his own personality.

He started training his pups when they were just three weeks old, developing a trusting relationship. *No trust, no team.*

He told me about one of his favorite dogs, Zazz. She was badly injured as a pup when Frank's father backed over her legs. They flew her to Vancouver for surgery. When she came home she had no hair on her hind leg, so she spent the winter in his cabin. Who knows what helped Zazz's recovery—probably the family interactions. Frank never expected her to be part of a sled team, but he felt she was a great family dog with a full heart. But Zazz ran his lead for several years in competitive Quests.

There was a message here. Never give up; anyone could be a winner.

Frank evaluated his puppies by giving each a chance to perform. He told me that what he looked for was "attitude, attitude, and attitude." He never eliminated a dog as a possibility to run. "You never know at what age one will surface to excel," he told me. He looked for the unique formula for each individual dog—what would drive the dog to succeed—and then he offered consistency.

For Frank, equipment could be the weak point. He bought only the best.

Another critical lesson was not to overload a leader; contributors are just as necessary for the team and deserve equal respect.

Frank's goal was not to achieve maximum performance, but optimum performance. He didn't want to be greedy; he just wanted to succeed at a level, consistent mark.

Asked what it takes to win, he modestly replied, "Excellent preparation, implementation of a plan, making the right decision at the right time while having things go your way." The preparation encompasses training and planning, implementation is the action item, and having things go your way could involve the universe's intervention.

He mentioned one last, very important concept, which was not to be afraid to *go for it* with a strong belief in your team (your security to venture forth, confidence, courage).

Maybe Frank's survival is predicated on the animals, his listening, and his connection to the spirit of nature.

To Win the Game

*The bottom line is this: why do some people survive
and some don't? Why are some immobilized with
fear, crippled by panic, while others are filled with
strength, endurance, and the ability to act? What
actually makes the difference, and how do you win?*

IT IS OBVIOUS AS I REREAD MY STORIES OF people from all walks of life and experiences—with varied emotional, physical, and preparedness abilities—that we are all warriors just trying to make it in life. Some fight more than others. Some receive more from nurturing parents and experiences. Some are smarter in the ways that count. And some receive more support from friends, acquaintances, and family. And then there are those who welcome a spiritual guide into their struggle to bring them through.

Some individuals end up losing. They may be unable to accept the clues presented and unwilling to adapt with solutions that would deal with their stresses. They may not have an active support channel.

Why do survivors win?

Natural instincts influence our survival. According to the *U.S. Army Survival Manual*, fear, anxiety, frustration, anger, depression, loneliness, and guilt greatly affect a person's likelihood of survival. In these stages we go through to deal with challenging occurrences, we must find a way to adapt to our changing world.

Fear is the first stage in a crisis. Sometimes fear can be positive, moving a person forward in a cautious manner to avoid injury. Yet fear also immobilizes a person. It can rob action. Fear influences the circuitry in our brain. The good news is that people can train to overcome fear, to achieve a secondary response and move forward. This is something taught in the military.

Courage is key to conquering fear. I've written extensively about this in my book *Courage Quest*. Courage is a skill that you can develop daily, so that when a need arises, you are prepared with a response that is automatic, almost instinctual. As you learn to face risk and make a plan, you can quickly overcome obstacles.

Anxiety develops from fear and can affect your physical, mental, and emotional responses. It makes it difficult to think or make judgments. Anxiety can immobilize you.

You then become frustrated from not being able to reach a goal. In order to survive, a person needs to stay alive—either by finding help or by devising their own way out of a situation. It is imperative to call on resources and all of your wonderful life assets at this point—everything you have learned and the emotional support of friends and family.

If your plan fails and you cannot find a solution, your frustration is often accompanied by anger.

Anger comes from not having access to resources for survival, and it can produce irrational responses. To get past this, you must move through that feeling and toward a more productive action. You must focus, use your energy, and not waste unnecessary energy.

Depression can consume you. It is normal in a stressful situation. Emotions are now linked to your frustration and anger, and your inability to achieve. You become worn to your core and may wish to quit trying. A feeling of hopelessness and loss of energy emerge.

Thinking about loved ones can energize and comfort you then trigger movement forward. This may be the time to be creative and use your imagination in a positive way. Survivors are able to tap their inner strength and fortitude, and keep their minds active. This can fight depression. Self-sufficiency brings with it confidence and the capability to move forward alone.

Loneliness surfaces, and boredom follows.

Guilt could enter the mix. When others have suffered, some people may wonder why they themselves have been spared. It can be a beneficial emotion, encouraging them to move forward with life, but others give up. Some purpose, a higher reason, may surface to provide the impetus to continue fighting. The important thing is to feel there is a reason for life and fight actively for it.

What do survivors do?

Survivors store what they learn through life, which helps them in a crisis situation. They act on the information they acquire, paying attention to their intuition and instincts.

They are humble, know when to rest, and understand when it is wise to be afraid. They don't go beyond their capabilities. They have humility and are adaptable. Anger motivates and pushes them forward.

Hormones produced under stress change your thinking. This actually causes increased adrenaline flow. Stress limits your focus and makes thinking difficult. Risk takers, who often push through their stress, exhibit courage with a playful sense of humor. They are curious and adaptable. They listen to their intuition and instincts, and they are independent thinkers. Rule breakers, they defy authority and do what feels best. They face reality with a positive attitude and are able to access the big picture.

A 2012 article in *Forbes* talked about what makes a person a success. The author stated that it was not necessarily a person's intelligence, but skills that involve "human engineering"—a measurement of how you communicate, negotiate, and lead. Likeability and trust are built from emotional, moral, and body intelligence. This can help you survive in any situation.

John F. Kennedy, for example, had an intelligence quotient (IQ) of only 119, while Madonna's is reportedly 140. IQ measurement is used as an indicator of logical reasoning and technical intelligence. It is often considered by businesses today when hiring, but it is not a good indicator of competence and achievement.

Frequently people who survive believe in a higher power, act altruistically, and display strong feelings of empathy. They have a supportive family and community ties. They do not dwell on the past, but are forward looking.

Most importantly, they have a strong will to live, with a purpose and a vision for the future.

How do survivors win?

Winning at this survival game requires many actions. I have highlighted lessons from previous stories:

After Michael and I kayaked in Alaska I began my journey of discovery to learn what drives a person to survive. Using these stories as a guide, I now have a clearer picture of how we handled our own threatening situation.

Why did we embark on this difficult, isolated trip in terrible weather? Why didn't we recheck our equipment on a journey where equipment is critical, and why didn't we use the heat and food on the raft?

We made some good decisions. Our fear, and later our anger, moved us into action. I remained calm, and my past experience on solo backpacking trips allowed me to handle my emotions and devise a plan. Unloading and lifting the kayak to the floating raft was smart. In retrospect, Michael was probably right to want to paddle to the sailboat. I did not want to change my original plan and thought we should continue, but pushing ahead in a dangerous situation, ill prepared, is often the reason people die in extreme circumstances.

Fate also intervened, putting that sailboat that would never have been in our waters had it not been for their engine trouble. We got lucky (the word I hear from many survivor stories), and that turned the course of our events.

Larry, the packer caught in a mountain storm, was aware of how things affected him, and he kept his feelings, thoughts, and actions in control. He took small steps as he evaluated information, weighing risks while on his dangerous trek out of the wilderness. With bold actions, risking but cautious, he moved down the mountain. Somehow, he knew he would make it. He remained mentally strong and positive, a lover of life; he took responsibility and didn't acknowledge failure was possible. Disillusionment is an easy trap for a lost person to fall into, as your mind plays with you. The answer is to look within for self-balance and solutions. Mental strength was a trait also of Frank Turner, the musher, and many of the other survivors showed.

Lane, the smokejumper, was dealt two bad hands but pushed through to stand tall. He assessed his physical injuries as soon as he regained consciousness; he straightened his own broken leg in a situation where every minute made a difference in how it would heal. He remained calm, letting his increased adrenaline control his pain as he put his energy to work, aided by his experience and training. He used his energy to accomplish two phenomenal recoveries.

During his hospital time, Lane looked at death, rejected it, and played with visual images. For some unknown reason, this brought him out of his coma. He saw wondrous out-of-body visualizations, and made them his friends. He proved others wrong when they thought he would die, and he proved that anything is possible. The people who have the best chance of survival are those who have a strong image of what is happening outside their immediate world; in Lane's case, that meant his out-of-body experiences.

My mom has some of the same qualities as Lane. She's persistent in her battle, with an extraordinary will to live.

She also plays with visual images in her confined state, and she's accepted her life and moved forward. Her curiosity enriches her mind. Frequent calls with her children give her a purpose to live, as she supports them from afar. Often seeing the humorous side of life's situations, Mom is able to balance and control the emotions of her confinement.

Ed struggled to return from his coma and his rehabilitation regiment. Like Lane, he was persistent, positive, and would not accept death. His family may have been the reason for his survival, along with the mystical angel visiting to reassure him he could stay a bit longer here on earth. Ed's one tough fellow, able to explore a new path in life. He now blossoms with full wonder and exhibits gratitude with a new softening of emotions.

Writing the stories of the premature babies, I saw two infants whose lives were possibly gifts from angels to their families. They were supported by their guardians, the family members who loved them beyond description, and those who sent positive energy and acted daily to promote the babies' battle to live. Those tiny babies developed internal strength that is obvious today as they move through life. Despite some restrictions, they overcome and prosper, enriching society.

Annette Herfkens was thrown into a world others would view as a horror movie. Most people would give up when everyone else, including a loved one, had already died beside them. Unable to move or find food, yet with her persistence in living, Annette adapted to what was possible in her realm, and soaked up the lifesaving water. She remained calm despite the jungle creatures devouring the bodies around her and put her mind in a place of safety and bliss. Her transformation continues today as she explores what happened in that jungle.

Brianna Karp focused on a balanced life with persistence and a belief in the future. This woman hoped to continue and improve her circumstances. With a positive attitude, remaining open to possibilities, she explored various solutions to homelessness until doors of opportunity opened. She was willing to adapt to each new challenge, and that became more important than her original plan; adaptability always assists people in survival. Sometimes ideas drive action and become as powerful as emotions when overcoming situations.

Alicia Blatz, submerged when the bridge collapsed, also looked death in the face, saw its beauty, but decided she wanted to live. She fought valiantly, conquering her struggles.

Survivors often discover an internal core of strength, faith, or a reason they fight to live. A spirit will enter their struggles, as we heard from Ed after his prolonged coma and Garett Ebling who survived the bridge collapse. Their struggles were possibly greater than their past abilities to overcome, and they found their solutions through a higher power. Those moments became a turning point, a wake-up call, and a chance to welcome something new in each person's life.

Amal Elsana Alh'jooj was frustrated and angry about her restrictions as a woman in a dusty settlement in Israel. This moved her forward to find solutions not only for herself, but for her community. Determined, she persisted, taking small steps at first, which moved her eventually to leaps. She started an integrated school for young children, taught community women to read, and began to travel to receive awards and speak at engagements. For her, the risk was necessary for females to survive and flourish in their environments.

Eleanor Smithwick also showed a commitment to her cause. She never gave up on her clinic by the Amazon River, assisting indigenous people and helping to liberate women from their subservient status to men. Exposed to disease and defiant attitudes, Eleanor has persevered. She is one of my personal heroes, saving many lives. A survivor!

During the Foxtrot 586 crash, some men lived and some died, but their story reveals the heroes who saved the lives of others. The survivors lived because of their sharpened senses; most had families to live for, and their adrenaline and military training kicked in. They kept moving, never allowing themselves to fall asleep in the cold water. Faith also was an important component in their will to live. Most of the men who died were confused, exhausted, dehydrated, and could not control their anxiety. The pilot, however, died after saving others. The strong lived.

Danelle Ballengee was amazing. She resisted shutting down or retreating after her accident in the canyon, but insistently crawled forward. Danelle lived in the present, not looking at the past—which is always out of our control—or the future, which is unpredictable.

Ernest Shackleton, during his brutal struggle in Antarctica, considered his men to be a team. He praised their accomplishments and encouraged participation in exploring ideas together. But when there were important decisions to be made, he listened to his own inner voice, mulled over the options, and made his own call about how to move forward. He was not attempting to please others as he led his team to safety. He helped those who were struggling—for instance, the man who needed his gloves. In doing so, he focused on another's needs and lessened his fears in the giving.

What are the keys to survival?

When a traumatic event strikes, it is difficult to focus. However, it's important to listen actively, calming yourself before you make important decisions and not allowing yourself to feel overwhelmed. It's difficult to do this in emotional conflicts. Anytime you can allow humor into your situation, it will help alleviate your anxiety, frustration, and fear. Also, look at the basis of the problem and eliminate information that is not important for decision making. Limit physical exertion; operate at 60 percent of normal and only employ physical action when there will be a positive outcome.

How do some lose?

In crisis, people die of confusion. They fail to calmly analyze their situation, and exhaustion, dehydration, hypothermia, anxiety, hunger, and injury ensue.

Some of the people I highlighted in the previous stories were struggling, with little hope for a positive outcome. They seemed to be headed in the direction of destruction. What might have helped them survive? They seemed to be losing the game. I searched for answers to their plights and how they might recover, but saw little hope at the stages where they were.

The family in the campground lost their self-control as their apathy led to psychological deterioration and spun them into confusion. Their judgment deteriorated, and they lived in denial, operating on many misperceptions of rescue, just as Kiki did in the Greek hostel. Their finances eroded. There are government subsidy programs, and their families had offered help, but pride took its toll.

Kiki suffered from many of the problems that plague people who cannot flourish. I think she, too, was in the denial phase, and she hadn't budged from it ever since her partner kicked her out of their home years before. She languished as a result. Unable to take charge, and as depression surfaced, she seemed indifferent, illogical, and irrational in her assessment of her current situation. She often dwelt on the past, thinking her partner would change and support her. She created a world she desired when she couldn't handle the difficulty of her present, and then became impatient and agitated as her resources disappeared. Survivors do not look at themselves as victims, but a non-survivor complains and expects to be rescued. Kiki had lost herself.

During Robert Scott's Antarctic expedition, just as everything went wrong and the men died, Scott's mind was living in previous times. He vividly remembered the comforts and safety of home. This was dangerous, as it moved him beyond his current sensibilities and cautions.

He was depressed about another explorer claiming the South Pole. This defeat, embedded in his mind, was the beginning of the end as he started to give in to fear, leaving him less able to cope with the obstacles facing his team. His emotion overtook his logical mind. He miscalculated places, distances, and the energy required to achieve his goals, which led his team to haul those heavy rock samples to the bitter end. The men expended too much energy pulling those sleds, especially with frostbite and meager rations. They were hungry and stressed, just as Kiki in the hostel, and could no longer make productive decisions.

When I was working in Silicon Valley in the 1990s, I was privileged to attend a leadership seminar taught by Stephen R. Covey. The course, *The 7 Habits for Success*, has beneficially influenced my life ever since, and I still review some of his messages daily.

In essence, Covey suggested there are seven habits that are most important for effective performance and happiness. They reminded me of some of the principles I heard while staying with Frank Turner and learning about his Yukon dogsled operation.

Covey's seven habits are:

- Be *proactive* (we are responsible for our own lives)
- *Begin with the end in mind* (envision end result)
- *First things first* (see what you want and make it happen)
- *Independence* (find a solution with team members, but continue your own direction for decisions)

- *Seek first to understand* (empathetic listening)
- *Synergize* (positive teamwork to achieve goal)
- *Sharpen the saw* (balance your life resources and health)

We can acquire knowledge, desire, and skill. Life requires balance, and these habits create one of our keys to successful survival—something we can draw upon in difficult, life-threatening circumstances.

Practice may also be a component in saving lives. With repeated actions, soon your reaction becomes automatic, happening at a subconscious level. You can visualize the outcome of a particular task. The stages people go through in disasters, starting with denial and moving through panic and paralysis, can be shortened to allow you to act sooner.

With growth, change, constant improvement, and practice, you will create an upward spiral of learning, commitment, and doing. This will prepare you to react instinctively when a survival challenge arrives.

We need to have a mission in life—a sense of what is truly important to us. Many times it is our family or our wish to do and be better. A mission creates our will to survive and directs us in threatening situations.

I've learned about survival while writing this book. My conclusions are not what I expected when I embarked on this journey. They are important lessons. We must care for our fellow man as we do ourselves, and pull them into our boat. The spiritual influence I dismissed in the beginning of my search is real, powerful, and should not be ignored. There's not one thing that saves us, but instead a combination of the physical, emotional, and spiritual resources.

Why should we care about survival, other than remaining in the present world?

This question came to me at the culmination of this project. Sure, we can live longer, but I would like to live better. I want to learn to survive with grace. That now seems to be a higher, more altruistic benefit. By growing, we can expand our horizons of future possibilities. It necessitates conquering our fears through courage, acknowledging our connection to our worldwide race, knowing that we are equal and that each person deserves our assistance. There is a need to be prepared for the unexpected.

The survival keys my heroes experienced, and what I've discovered through my writing, come down to this:

The ordinary can do the extraordinary.

My hope is that we can learn how to live full lives, not fearing how to survive but knowing how to.

Many of these suggestions are evident in the stories I've told about the winners and losers. People who survive are continually challenged in life, but each time they rebound with the same spirit. A survivor is a survivor, and there is a prerequisite—having courage to risk—that allows them to engage in these adventures. We must allow ourselves the freedom to fail. We can always remount.

Here are some questions that will begin your own search for survival:

- Can a life-threatening crisis become a gift that feeds you going forward?
- What part does surrender and acceptance play, along with the spiritual, in survival?
- How important is your will to live? Do you have a plan, a persistence, the support and love you need?
- What is survival to you? Is it more than just remaining alive, on earth?
- Do people survive on guts alone?
- What part in survival do zest, a desire to connect with others, and improving humanity play?

Acknowledgements

Great thanks to:

My editor, Beth Jusino, who gently guided me through this process with her questions that only I could answer.

My good friend Dania, who always listened and, with her poetic quality of life, always guided.

Jenn Reese, for listening to my intention and designing just the right book cover.

My daughter, who understood, without me explaining, that her crazy mom was off doing her thing, writing another book, and sometimes couldn't be disturbed.

The garden of friends and acquaintances who encouraged me, saying, "I just can't wait to read this book."

Keith Snyder, whose words ring in my ears daily: "Put your butt down in the seat and write."

My guides, whose willingness to selflessly relinquish their stories of survival to assist others in their search to live a full life.

And when it became difficult to write one more word, when I was tired and spent, those darn angels who kept encouraging and reminding me of balance.

My Research

Chapter 2
White Wilderness Expedition

- Gilford, Judith. *The Packing Book*. September 1, 2006.
- Smoke, Elsner and Bill Brown. *Packin' in on Mules and Horses*. 1980.
- Copyboy Heaven Consulting. *Horse Packing. www.cowboyhvn. com/Horse_Packing.htm*.

Chapter 4
Free-Falling Lane

- MESA, AZ Medical & Healing. *Riverside Trauma Conference— Lamoreaux presentation.* January 31, 2013.
- Grote, Tom. Star News. *Fall Down Two Times, Get Up Three— Lane.* July 10, 2014.
- You Tube—Lane Lamourauex blog. *Paragliding and Accident.* https://www.youtube.com/user/TravelLane.
- Lane Lamourauex blog. *Help Lane Lose The Cane. www. helplanelosethecane.com*.

Chapter 6
Down on Their Luck

- Dolan, Karen. EHRP, Economic Hardship Reporting Project, Peter Edelman on "Why It's So Hard to End Poverty in America." May 29, 2012. *economichardship.org/peter-edelman-on-why-its-so-hard-to-end-poverty-in-america/*.

- *Scott, Elizabeth, M.S. about health. Stress. May 11, 2013.* stress. about.com/od/financialstress/a/poverty.htm.

Chapter 7
A Lost Soul

- Wikipedia. *Greek government debt crisis 2000.* en.wikipedia.org/ wiki/Greekgovernment-debt_crisis.
- Wikipedia. *Greek debt crisis timeline.* en.wikipedia.org/wiki/... sovereign_debt_crisis_timeline.

Chapter 8
The Miracle

- *Huffington Post. Coma—You Can Be Completely Mentally Alert While In A Coma. www.huffingtonpost.com/news/coma/.*
- Wikipedia. *Coma. https://en.wikipedia.org/wiki/Coma.*
- Science Blog. *Washington University School of Medicine. Women more likely than men to have a stroke after heart surgery.* April 2000. *www3.scienceblog.com/community/older/2001/F/200116077. html.*

Chapter 9
A Preemie's Struggle

- Wikipedia. *Preterm Birth. https://en.wikipedia.org/wiki/Preterm_ birth.*

Chapter 10
Can I Survive the Jungle?

- Bryant, Charles W. Howstuffworks. *adventure.howstuffworks.com/ survival/wilderness/live-without-food-and-water3.htm.*
- *Herfkens, Annette. Turbulence. 2014. The Story. www. annetteherfkens.com/.*

Chapter 11
Homeless Girl

- Muszynski, Stuart. THE BLOG. HUFF POST—Education. *If life is a game, what are the rules?* November 21, 2014. *www. huffingtonpost.com/stuart-muszynski/if-life-is-a-game-what-ar_b_6199132.html.*

- Karp, Brianna. Blog: *The Girl's Guide to Homelessness. girlsguidetohomelessness.com/about/.*

- Karp, Brianna. Brianna's background three days into homelessness. February 23, 2009. *girlsguidetohomelessness. com/2009/02/23/initiation/.*

- *Ennion, Jennifer. www.*news.com.au. *How Girl's Guide to Homelessness blogger Brianna Karp's life has changed.* January 3, 2012. *www.news.com.au/technology/how-girls-guide-to-homelessness-blogger-brianna-karps-life-has-changed/story-e6frfro0-1226235960256.*

Chapter 12
Bridge Collapse

- Wikipedia. *I-35W Mississippi River Bridge. https://en.wikipedia. org/wiki/I-35W_Mississippi_River_bridge.*

- Star Tribune. *ww2.startribune.com/projects/bridge/carList_Cdata. xml. (there are interesting statements from survivors).*

- CNN. *The Story.* August 3, 2007. *www.cnn.com/2007/ US/08/03/bridge.collapse/photos.html.*

- Postuma, Sarama. St. Michael Patch. *Collapse of 35W Bridge Left Mark on St. Michael Mother, Survivor.* August 2, 2012.

- patch.com/minnesota/stmichael/five-years-later-a-st-michael-mom-shares-her-story.

Chapter 13
Woman's Struggle—Negev

- Wikipedia. *Negev Bedouin Women. https://en.wikipedia.org/wiki/ Negev_Bedouin_women.*

- Human Rights and Human Welfare. *Bedouin Women in the Naqab, Israel: Ongoing Transformation. www.du.edu/korbel/hrhw/researchdigest/mena/Bedouin.pdf.*

- Goldhill, Olivia. The Telegraph. *Bedouin's story: nomadic women can be feminists too.* November 28, 2013.

- *www.telegraph.co.uk/women/womens-life/10480943/A-Bedouins-story-nomadic-women-can-be-feminists-too.html.*

- YouTube presentation from Amal Elsane Alh'jooj. *Insisting on Equality.* https://www.youtube.com/watch?v=P-joysawaAU.

- Guntaj, Nir. www.ynetnews.com. *Bedouin women in Israel are still being circumcised.* July 15, 2008. *www.ynetnews.com/articles/0,/340,L-3568416,00.htm.*

- Cwikel, Julie; Lev-Wiesel; Rachel, Al-Krenawi, Alean. Sage Journals. February, 2003. Ben-Gurion University of the Negev. *The Impact of High Fertility and Pervasive Domestic Violence. vaw.sagepub.com/content/9/2/240.short.*

- Goldhill, Olivia. The Telegraph. *A Bedouin's story: nomadic women can be feminists too.* November 28, 2013. *www.telegraph.co.uk/women/womens-life/10480943/A-Bedouins-story-nomadic-women-can-be-feminists-too.html.*

- Corbett, Sarah. (photographer Stephanie Sinclair). The New York Times. *A Cutting Tradition.* January 22, 2008.

- www.nytimes.com/2008/01/20/magazine/20circumcision-t.html?_r=0.

- Wikipedia. *Female Genital Mutilation.* https://en.wikipedia.org/wiki/Female_genital_mutilation.

- Lowen, Linda. *Woman Inequality, Gender Gap: Feminist Movement and Equal Rights.* About News. *Facts About Women. womensissues.about.com/od/feminismequalrights/a/Top10FactsAboutWomen.htm.*

- *Wikipedia. The Feminist Movement.* en.wikipedia.org/wiki/Feminist_movement.

Chapter 14
Crash in Enemy Water

- Jampoler, Andrew C. A. Readers Digest short story. Navy Safety Center. *ADAK, The Rescue of Alfa Foxtrot 586.* September, 1979.

- Jampoler Andrews C.A. Book. *ADAK. The Rescue of Alfa Foxtrot 586.* November, 2011.

- Patton, Charlie. The Florida Times Union. *The Rescue of Alpha Foxtrot 586.* September 23, 2003. (Jampoler is a retired naval aviator and former commanding officer of Patrol Squadron 19 of the Nava Air Station, Moffett Field).

Chapter 15
Canyon Runner

- Darlow Smithson Productions series, aired on the Discovery Channel, *I Shouldn't be Alive.* Discovery Channel.

- tvweb.com/shows/i-shouldnt-be-alive/season-2/nightmare-canyon-aka-life-or-death-in-frostbite-canyon.

- Runner's World. *Danelle Ballengee—5 Years later.* December 12, 2011. www.runnersworld.com/.../danelle-ballengee-five-years-later.

Chapter 16
Antarctica Assaults – Shackleton:

- Roberts, David. An Outside Book—Outside Magazine. Great Exploration Stories. *Points Unknown.* 2000.

- Three part PBS series. Raw TV producers. *Chasing Shackleton (The Expedition).* 2013.

- Wikipedia. *Shackleton. https://en.wikipedia.org/wiki/Ernest_Shackleton.*

- *Childhood—Ernst Shackleton.* ehshackleton.weebley.com/childhood.html.

- The James Caird Society. *Shackleton.* htp://www.ernestshackleton.co.uk/shackleton/early-life/.

- *Antarctic Explores: Ernest Shackleton. www.south-pole.com/p0000098.htm.*

- Mann, John F. *The Endurance Obituaries. www.enduranceobituaries.com.uk/thedogs.htm.*

Apsley Cherry-Garrard:

- Wikipedia. *The Worst Journey in the World.* https://en.wikipedia.org/wiki/The_Worst_Journey_in_the_World.
- Christie's The Art People. *British Antarctica Expedition 1910-1913.* www.christies.com/lotfinder/books-manuscripts/british-antarctic-expedition-1910-1913-apsley-george-5605364-details.aspx.
- Apsley Cherry-Garrard quotes. *www.azquotes.com/quote/792513.*

Robert Falcon Scott:

- Ward, Paul. Cool Antarctica. *Robert Falcon Scott—The Journey to the Pole.* coolantarctica.com/Antarctica%20fact%20file/History/Robert-Falcon-Scott2.php.
- Wikipedia. *Robert Falcon Scott.* https://en.wikipedia.org/wiki/Robert_Falcon_Scott.
- *Scott's Last Expedition.www.scottslastexpedition.org/expedition/robert-falcon-scott.*

Chapter 17
Learning from the Master of Yukon Quest

- Muktuk Kennels. *Meeting Yukon Champion Frank Turner.* muktuk.com.
- Yukon Quest Website. *Frank Turner.* www.yukonquest.com.
- Sled Dog Watchdog Yukon News. *Meet Yukon Quest Champion Frank Turner.* 2007. www.sleddogcentral.com/interviews/turner.htm.
- Yukon Quest Mushing Gear. *iditarad.com.*
- Muktuk Adventures. www.muktuk.com.

Chapter 18
To Win the Game

- Keld, Jensen. Forbes. Leadership article. *Intelligence is overrated: What You Really Need To Succeed.* April 12, 2012.
- U.S. Army Survival Manual. *Types of National Instincts.*
- Covey, Dr. Stephen. *Worldwide Lessons in Leadership Series.*

About the Author

Sally DeMasi grew up in New York, earning her bachelor of science with some studies in Siena, Italy. Upon graduating, she immediately struck out for California in search of adventures.

After her stint in the California high-tech industry, in 2001 she found her life home in the small, pristine town of McCall, Idaho. Her paradise includes a pearl of a lake and outdoor opportunities like mountain climbing, rafting, kayaking, camping, and skiing. It gives Sally the ideal place to experience real living and her art.

Now she is free to explore her love of writing and photography.

Sally is the author of *Courage Quest,* in which she reaches out to encourage women and men to bolster their courage and expand their lives through positive self-image, and to reap the treasures this allows. The book details some of her solo international adventure travels and includes photos from her search for courage. She travels with a small backpack, staying in hostels, moving on public transportation or on foot, conquering her fears, and exploring the cultures of the world.

Her photos can be enjoyed at exhibits and in books, newspapers, and upscale galleries as well as on her blogs. A versatile artist, she pushes the envelope exploring new territory, creating vibrant impressionistic/fauvism art, and recently, abstract works with a painterly quality.

Contact Sally
Your questions and comments are welcome!

Email Sally at *sallydemasi4@gmail.com*

Visit Sally's blog for each of her books, including inspirational posters, photos, cards, and calendars:

www.couragequest.net
www.SurvivalSpiritualQuest.com

For Sally's blog of photography and stories:

www.sallydemasi.com

You might also be interested in Sally DeMasi's book

COURAGE QUEST

A story of courage — Sally's first quest for discovery

Travel along on her journeys as she explores the world on her own, pack on her back, facing fears during her search.

70446058R00159

Made in the USA
Columbia, SC
07 May 2017